SPIRITUAL POWER
How It Works

SPIRITUAL
POWER

How It Works

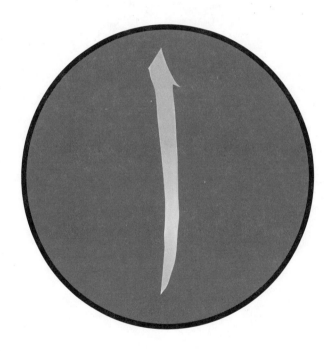

LLEWELLYN VAUGHAN-LEE

First published in the United States in 2005 by
The Golden Sufi Center
P.O. Box 428, Inverness, California 94937.

© 2005 by The Golden Sufi Center.

Printed and bound by Thomson-Shore, Inc.

Library of Congress Cataloging-in-Publication Data

Vaughan-Lee, Llewellyn.
Spiritual power : how it works / Llewellyn Vaughan-Lee.
    p. cm.
Includes bibliographical references (p.) and index.
ISBN 1-890350-11-7 (alk. paper)
  1. Spiritual life. I. Title

BL624.V3863 2005
297.4'4--dc22

                                        2005040390

CONTENTS

PREFACE

Throughout this book, in an effort to maintain continuity and simplicity of text, God, the Great Beloved, is referred to as He. Of course, the Absolute Truth is neither masculine nor feminine. As much as It has a divine masculine side, so It has an awe-inspiring feminine aspect.

INTRODUCTION

When you make the two one and
When you make the inner as the outer and the above
As below, and when
You make the male and the female into a single one
Then you shall enter the kingdom.

The Gospel of St. Thomas[1]

There was a time when every grove and stream was sacred, meaning and wisdom were found in the cycles of the moon and the germination of the plants. The divine was seen as present in everything from the fire on the hearth to the stars in the heavens. The earth was marked by lines of power, called "lay lines" in the West, "dragon lines" in the East. Where certain lines intersected, temples and circles of standing stones were built. These were places of power where spiritual energy was most concentrated and accessible. The power at these sites and their temples not only helped people in their relationship to the divine, but also aided the flow of spiritual energy into the whole of life. Through these places of power, nature was nourished, the crops grew, and the people benefitted both inwardly and outwardly, in their souls and in their daily lives.

The rise of monotheism with its image of a transcendent God banished the divine to heaven, and mankind was left alone on earth. The lines of power in the earth were forgotten, and although churches were often built on the ancient sacred sites, the esoteric knowledge of bringing their spiritual energy into life was lost. An all-embracing relationship to the divine was replaced by the knowledge of physical science. Crops became nourished by fertilizers and pesticides rather than ritual and prayer. The crops grew taller, but a spiritual nourishment faded from daily life.

Meanwhile religious life focused on our relationship with a transcendent God. The spires of the churches and the domes of the mosques raised our vision to heaven. And the message that was taught was often of personal salvation, looking forward to a heavenly life after death. Magic, the use of energy from the unseen, was banned by the church. Miracles belonged only to the hand of the one God or His saints, and those with healing power often had to work in secret. And these isolated acts of spiritual power worked primarily only at the level of the individual. The knowledge of what spiritual power is and how it can work as a system with the whole of life has been forgotten, except in some shamanic traditions.

Each age has its own knowledge. The matriarchal age understood the magic of the earth and the rhythms of life. The patriarchal era has given us the understanding and the limitations of science. In the coming era we will see something we have never seen before—the inner and outer will work together; the visible and unseen worlds will combine their energy and wisdom giving us the power and knowledge we need for the next era of our evolution. Part of this shift towards wholeness will be to take the spiritual out of the personal and transcendent arena and return it to all of creation. This will mean a reawakening of the knowledge of how spiritual power works in the world.

Our physical world needs to be purified and healed. Our systems of power are corrupt and do not serve the whole. We cannot move into the next era unless we embrace and live from a larger dimension of the spiritual.

The way that spiritual energy works in the inner and outer worlds is an exact science. Although it has been hidden for many centuries, this work has continued, practiced by certain spiritual masters and their helpers. They have held this wisdom for humanity, looked after the places of power and the flow of energy from the inner to the outer.

Shifts are currently taking place in the flow of this energy. Places of power that have been dormant are soon to be activated. If we are to participate in these changes for the benefit of the whole, we need the knowledge of how the energy works. We need to have an understanding not only about the places of power but also how their hidden potential can be utilized. This esoteric knowledge belongs to our heritage and to the need of the moment. It has a potency that is part of the awakening of the world.

At each time of transition there are those who will gladly step into the unknown, into the future that is being born. And there are those who will resist any change. It is for each of us to respond from the place within where we are free, where conditioning and fear does not grip us. Through our response we can make a real contribution to the changes that are taking place. This work with the energy of life is no longer for the select few, but for any who dare lift their face to the dawn. The price is that we leave behind our focus on personal well-being, both material and spiritual. The needs of the whole must be our primary concern. There is important work to be done at the place where the inner and outer meet, where the worlds come together. This work will determine the patterns of life in the coming era.

The unseen worlds have many secrets to share with us, but we must be able to receive them. We must be open to dimensions beyond our present understanding and allow these inner worlds to communicate with us. A bridge is being built between the worlds. This is not a rainbow bridge of bright colors and spiritual fantasy. It is built from the basic substance of this world combined with qualities of the inner worlds. The work on this bridge is almost finished. When it is complete, the inner and outer will be connected in a manner that will last far into the future. This bridge is being built in the midst of life, accessible from within our normal, everyday existence— it does not need esoteric knowledge to access it. Its connection between the worlds will enable humanity as a whole to be nourished directly from the inner in a new way—not dependent upon priests, shamans, or oracles, but accessible to the whole of humanity.

For each of us this bridge is our own individual connection to the inner world of the soul. Some can already see it in dreams, in painting or music. Others will sense it in a quality of joy returning to life, an ease of access to a depth of meaning in the ordinary. Through this connection magic will happen, the simple magic in which life comes alive and the unexpected happens. At this time knowledge will also be given, the knowledge of how the worlds work together, how inner and outer are bonded and interrelate. Many different forms of knowledge will come into the world, such as how light can be used to heal and transform, and how dreams work; some of the hidden qualities of matter will become known.

This bridge has been carefully made to withstand the aggression of disbelief and the power dynamics of control. Like the internet, this bridge belongs to the whole of humanity and no one group or individual will be able to control it. It is guarded by angels whose light belongs to God. It has been made by the masters of love and the forces behind creation. This bridge is a part of our heritage that has been recreated to serve the coming age. And it is a gift. There is no price to pay. Humanity has suffered enough.

This is not a dream; it belongs to the future that we are being given. It is made of the substance of life and the hopes of humanity. It is grounded in the ordinary and yet is full of the magic of each moment and the destiny of humankind. We are being asked to live it, to reconnect with what is highest, simplest, and most wonderful. It is for us to make it fully real.

This book belongs to the work of the future, the knowledge that is needed for our evolution. It is part of a tapestry that is being revealed in which certain colors and patterns are being shown for the first time. It cannot be understood solely on the level of the mind because the mind does not yet have the images or understanding that belongs to the future. There are as yet not many concepts for what is being given, no familiar frame of reference. But if there is a resonance with this knowledge, then connections are created, certain links between the inner and outer are formed, and a quality of understanding can be established. There is a new way to work with the patterns of life and the energy of the inner worlds. These chapters are a page in the book of the esoteric wisdom of the future.

SOURCES OF POWER

That boundless Power,
source of every power,
manifesting itself as life,
entering every heart,
that is Self.[1]

THE VEILING OF SPIRITUAL POWER

In the heart of the world there are sources of power needed for the evolution of humanity and the whole of the planet. Without this energy we will remain stuck at the dawn of the coming era, unable to step into the sunlight of the future. At present, the doors to these places of power are closed, inaccessible. And we remain distracted and dominated by the dynamics of physical and economic force.

Real power does not belong to humanity. It is a gift from the inner worlds and carries a stamp of the divine. It is given for the sake of the whole, not for our own personal gain. The next step in our evolution includes accessing this power, and using it to assist in the tremendous changes taking place in our world.

In order to access these places of power, we first need to understand why they are hidden. There are many reasons that power is hidden from humanity. Often it is to protect it from being used for the wrong reasons or by the wrong people. We know of the danger of the dynamics of power and domination, how easily power corrupts and is corrupted. Spiritual power, power which belongs to the nonphysical realm, is as corruptive as worldly power, and often more dangerous because it is invisible and not so easy to recognize or defend against.

Traditionally, only initiates have access to frequencies of spiritual power; the greater the power the more demanding the initiation. Supposedly these initiations rejected those who were not pure enough, only giving access to those who could not be corrupted. However, such safeguards are rarely perfect, and human nature is too complex for any safeguard to be fully effective.

Because our present culture's focus is on the physical world, we are familiar with the misuse of power that belongs to this dimension; we have little awareness of spiritual power or its misuse. We see economic and political corruption around us, as well as the underworld forces of drugs, prostitution, slavery, and other forms of human exploitation. Our history, present and past, tells stories of military power that has been used to dominate and enslave. There is also the dark history of religious power, including the Catholic Inquisition and other forms of religious intolerance. But all these forms of power still belong to the physical, material dimension. Even psychological manipulation mainly has its end in physical or material gain.

Spiritual power belongs to a different dimension, and is invisible to someone who sees only the physical world. But this power is real and has a vast range of possibilities. Traditionally it can be used locally, to heal an individual, or in communities, for example to help the rains come. Or it can have a global dimension, involving the well-being and evolution of the whole. We can see the remains of past cultures that used spiritual power in the pyramids of Egypt or the stone circles of England. We may have lost the knowledge of how spiritual energies were channeled through these monuments, but we can sense their mystery and potency.

If the new era that is now being born around us is to come into fruition it needs spiritual power, on not just an individual but also a global scale. Many spiritual traditions and practices have given individuals a taste of spiritual energies that can free them from the prison of a solely physical, material life and open them to other dimensions. But if the future is to be for the whole of humanity and not just a spiritual elite, then we need to find the sources of power that can transform the whole— give the whole of humanity access to a different dimension, a different way of life. Without these sources of power the transition that is beginning will stagnate. It will not move beyond the individual.

These sources of power are present, but hidden. They have been protected from misuse and the dangers of corruption. And there are even forces that resist their discovery. But the time has come for them to be uncovered and used.

MASTERS OF WISDOM

We need to reclaim spiritual power and learn how to use it. But how can we access it when we have forgotten its existence? How can we reclaim this power when it has been so carefully veiled? If we accept the existence of spiritual power, then we will need to accept that there are those among us who know how to use it.

In the last era in the West, matter was separated from spirit and the deity was imaged as a paternalistic figure in heaven, a spiritual realm accessible after death. The magi, the initiates who were masters of the inner worlds,

witnessed the birth of Christ. But the Christian priest-
hood preferred temporal to spiritual power, and those
who had direct access to the spiritual dimensions, like the
Gnostics, were persecuted. The masters who knew how
to use real spiritual power in this world wisely became
hidden. As these spiritual masters veiled themselves, the
knowledge of places of power and their use also became
veiled; knowledge of their existence remained only in
spiritual folklore.

Humanity busied itself with its material pursuits,
and the spiritual was understood as belonging to a different reality from everyday life. Power became associated
with might and domination, rather than understood as
a source of energy that belongs to all of life, to be used for
its benefit. Even when the industrial revolution brought
us new forms of energy, such as electricity, their cost was
the exploitation of nature and clouds of pollution. The
notion of a power that is free and pure no longer belongs
to our world. When we banished the spiritual dimension
to heaven, we also exiled ourselves from the purity and
freedom of its power.

The masters of wisdom, those who know how to use
spiritual power, have remained among us. They are hidden in their apparent ordinariness. They do not need the
trappings of worldly power, whose encumbrances could
interfere with their work. Wealth or recognition holds
no attraction for those who have passed beyond the
confines of the ego and work for the well-being of humanity. If their knowledge and ability are to become
known, it will mean a shift for them and their work.
But they have been preparing for this transition. They
have been slowly lifting the veils of protection that have
kept them hidden. They are working more visibly in the
world.

Yet the unveiling of these spiritual masters could easily upset the balance of worldly power. How can there be those among us who have access to a quality of power that is so different from all of our present images and concepts of power? Our worldly leaders pride themselves on their positions of worldly power and their ability to wield it. The structure of our civilization, our world order, is centered around their roles. This structure would be severely disturbed by the acknowledgment of a different level of power that does not belong to the dynamics of worldly domination, but to the ideal of spiritual servanthood.

In the matriarchal era preceding the patriarchal era, spiritual power was in the hands of the priestesses. Some of the patriarchy's fear and persecution of the feminine can be traced to these ancestral memories. Much of the power used by the priestesses belonged to the ways of nature, its beneficial nourishing and healing qualities. Remnants of their wisdom can be found in the feminine lore of herbs and other forms of healing. It also had a dark side in the knowledge of poisons and spells. But there were deeper places of power belonging not just to the magic of the land but also to the movement of the stars and the patterns of creation. The priestesses understood the relationship between spirit and matter and how the energies of the inner and outer worlds interrelate. Shamanic traditions have kept alive some of this knowledge, but most has been lost.

When the soldiers of the emerging patriarchy killed the priestesses and destroyed their temples, their swords also helped break the bond between spirit and matter. Our understanding of the fluid, creative relationship between outer and inner, physical and nonphysical, which belongs to the feminine wholeness was sacrificed by their violence and domination.

As God retreated from earth to heaven, He took His power with Him. The priests still acknowledge the existence of divine power, but they lost the wisdom of how to use it. Sometimes we respect His might in the forces of nature that we cannot control, the hurricane or earthquake, or see His wonder in unexplained miracles. But we remain the children of our image of God, the victims of His beneficent or destructive energies. The idea of working together with such powerful forces has slipped from our memories.

Our image of an omnipotent God has ignored the role of His servants, those who have passed beyond the *maya* of creation and the limitations of the ego to give themselves in service. Some of His servants have been trained to work with His power, to function as intermediaries between His omnipotence and the needs of humanity. In the Sufi tradition they are known as the *awiliyâ*, the friends of God.

There have been some periods in our recorded history when we have remembered that real power belongs to God and those who are in service to God. In the eleventh, twelfth, and thirteenth century the *Khwâjagân*, or masters of wisdom, had great influence among the peoples of Central Asia. These predecessors of the Naqshbandi Sufi masters were known to have great spiritual power and wisdom, and even the worldly rulers valued their help and guidance. But recent history tells few stories of such cooperation. There have been tribal cultures who were guided by their shamans, and there is the unique example of Tibet, ruled for centuries by the reincarnations of the Dalai Lama according to spiritual principles and rituals. But a ruler having real spiritual power does not belong to the struggles of the last two thousand years, where physical force and might in battle have been the dominant forces. We may acknowledge divine power in our private prayers, and acknowledge that some events may be due to the will of God. But we have no real understanding of how His power can play a part in world affairs. God and His power belong mainly in heaven, and we are left on earth with our own struggles.

THE KNOWLEDGE OF SPIRITUAL POWER

Spiritual power is real. Many spiritual students will have experienced some form of spiritual power on their quest, particularly when they encounter a real spiritual path or teacher. They sense an energy that is unlike anything they have known. It can have many qualities, a sweetness, light, an unexpected strength, a sense of something intangible that carries a presence. Often it is what attracts them to a path.

Unfortunately, many seekers are also deceived by what appears as spiritual power, mistaking personal magnetism, sexuality, psychological manipulation, or the subtle dynamics of codependency for a real inner experience. In the West our lack of understanding of the spiritual world has resulted in a naiveté that is easily exploited by someone pretending to have access to spiritual power. We also confuse psychic ability or clairvoyance with spiritual maturity. In our hunger for an experience beyond the physical we can get caught in spiritual illusions.

Spiritual power can be achieved through spiritual practice, or it can be given as a gift. Through spiritual practice the aspirant learns to access and channel certain energies from the inner planes. These energies are necessary for spiritual development, but they can also give the individual personal magnetism or other powers, for example the ability to read minds or see the patterns of future events. These are mainly low-level powers but they can be impressive to the uninitiated. Sometimes such powers can be used to manipulate or control others, even to accumulate wealth or worldly power.

But power that is still caught within the sphere of the ego is limited. There is a greater source of power that cannot be accessed by those trapped by the illusion of their own self. This is the power to which the masters of wisdom have traditionally had access, and which is used for the benefit of the whole. Like lesser forms of spiritual power, it belongs to the invisible inner world, but it has a very different quality and purpose.

This greater power cannot be achieved through effort. Severe spiritual discipline and practice are required, because the ego must not be allowed to interfere with its work. But the actual power is a gift. And there is a quality of freedom to this real power, because it is a reflection of That which is free, of That which cannot be limited. This power is rarely visible at work in the world.

Real spiritual power does not come from will or desire, but is a direct expression of an aspect of the divine. As such it carries a force and focus that belong to the Absolute, and have the stamp of divine will. Through spiritual power the will of the Absolute can be directly enacted in the world. This power does not have to follow the laws of creation because it belongs to the Creator. It is not caught in the patterns of cause and effect, by which most intentions become diluted or dispersed before they are fully enacted. When an intention is born in human consciousness, it enters the realm of duality, where there is a separation between intention and action. In the process of enacting an idea, the original purity of the idea inevitably becomes distorted. Shadow dynamics also interfere, which is where power dynamics enter. T.S. Eliot poignantly expresses this process:

Between the idea
And the reality
Between the motion
And the act
Falls the Shadow.[2]

However, real spiritual power does not belong to
the realm of duality or the dynamics of cause and effect.
It is born on the plane of pure being, or beyond, in the
uncreated emptiness. It has the capacity to interact with
creation without following the laws of creation, without
being caught by duality and its shadow dynamics. It is
often the lack of any shadow dynamic to this energy that
makes it invisible—we perceive things most easily by the
shadows they create. Light upon light is more difficult to
perceive than light upon darkness.

This spiritual energy that comes from beyond
duality, enacted by a master who has been made free from
the relative world, can come directly into life without
being caught in the play of opposites and its unfolding
dramas. It has the capacity to enact the will of the divine
in its simple essence. Something just happens. This is
what we call a miracle, when there is no logical cause,
no pattern of events that appears to cause something.
It just *is*. The divine enters life without the play of opposites, without following the process of creation. This
is what makes the intercession of the divine so simple
and potent.

Contrary to our conditioning, the intercession of
the divine is not caused by a father-figure God carefully
tending His children. There are more forces at work in
the beyond than we can imagine; there are beings of light
and beings of darkness that guide these forces and there
are laws which direct them in their work. There are, in
fact, very exact laws concerning the intercession of real

spiritual power. These laws follow very different principles from human laws that are bound by the play of duality, the apparent opposites of good and evil. For example, the laws of oneness cannot follow the principles of duality and the opposition of good and evil, because on the plane of oneness there is no such duality. And there are other laws in the uncreated worlds, in the realms of nonbeing through which the energy of the divine flows.

When the worlds are kept separate, the laws of one dimension do not interfere or interact with the laws of another. It is when different levels of reality come together, for example, when the dimension of oneness interacts with the plane of duality, that confusion can occur. Sometimes it may just seem that a miracle has occurred. But the intercession of a higher plane can also have seemingly negative effects, causing destruction or chaos, as for example when the biblical flood came and God cleansed a corrupted world.

We tend to think that God is good, but anyone who has passed beyond the images of dualism knows that the divine is not limited by human morality. There are depths of darkness in the divine that human conscious-ness cannot bear to encounter, just as there are dazzling rivers of light that would blind us. That is why these levels of reality are traditionally closed to the uninitiated. The trials and tests of spiritual initiation are needed to prepare our consciousness for these vaster horizons.

Humanity is protected from light that it cannot contain, from darkness that does not originate in igno-rance and greed. But sometimes there is a need for the beyond to break through our veils of protection and interact with human affairs. Often these interactions are themselves carefully veiled, so as not to disturb the illusions of humanity, of human beings' sense of self-determination. Containers are created in the inner and also in the outer world to give divine energy to humanity without overwhelming it. Some of the ancient monuments like the stone circles and pyramids served this purpose. Their patterns of sacred geometry and alignment with the magnetic power lines of the planet allowed the energy to flow from the inner to the outer with harmony. The priests of these sacred sites made sure that the inner and outer were kept in balance. Music that has a sacred dimension was also a vehicle for divine transmission, as were other sacred ceremonies.

Our knowledge of how these containers work, of how they nourished humanity with the energy of the inner world, has largely been lost. As our focus turned to the material world and our control of its natural sources of energy, we forgot how the inner and outer worlds interact. We became frightened of what we could not control, and labeled it as superstition. As humanity imaged a physical world separate from the spiritual, we enclosed ourself in the reality of our imaginings. The places of power became hidden, and certain doorways were closed. The energy of the divine was still present in life, nourishing us in secret ways, watched over by the friends of God and their helpers. But it was no longer part of our collective consciousness.

With many doorways to the divine closed, humanity had to work hard to survive, even creating an image of evolution as "survival." We have lost touch with the wonders of grace and the central miracle of life, that everything is a gift of God. That we are given all that we need by our Creator is not part of our present consciousness. Instead we have created our image of life as struggle, survival, and the politics of power. We have even forgotten that this is just an image of life that we have created.

THE FREEDOM OF SPIRITUAL POWER

The danger of any direct intercession of energy from the inner planes is that it does not belong to our collective conditioning. To explore the notion of spiritual power we have to step aside from our concepts of right and wrong, good and bad, and recognize that there are forces which we do not understand and cannot label. There is a freedom to this venture that will excite those bored with concepts, but with it will come the fear that arises when a certain safety is abandoned. And there is the deeper fear that we may actually encounter something that we cannot control. Even spiritual seekers condition their experience of their journey with images of the divine that fit into the safe framework of what they can control. An encounter with real spiritual power is rarely part of our spiritual imagination.

We are conditioned by images of worldly power, power that originates in our physical world. There is the obvious power that comes from physical force, or the more subtle power that comes from economic or other forms of domination. Another type of power comes from sources of energy: oil, coal, gas. Our present civilization depends upon these sources of energy, and they are a central factor in our economic and political power dynamics. But the central source of physical energy upon which we all depend, the sun, does not originate in this world. The sun has often been a symbol for the spiritual source of life. Sunlight gives energy to all of life and it is difficult to manipulate or control. Its energy is free of our worldly power dynamics. The difference between sunlight and other forms of power or energy illustrates the difference between spiritual and worldly power.

Sunlight is basic to life and is all around us; so is the spiritual energy that sustains us. Our understanding of how to use sunlight for domestic or industrial energy is still in its infancy. How to use spiritual energy in everyday life is a mystery to us. And yet this understanding is essential to our well-being. If we are to acknowledge the spiritual dimension of our being, that we need to be nourished by His light and love, then we need to become familiar with the power that originates in the inner worlds. This power can help to free us from the prison of our material existence and the fetters of worldly power. It can work in the world according to the will of God rather than the will of ego-identified individuals. By its nature it will benefit the whole of humanity rather than promote the dominance of particular groups or countries. Like the sunlight it is free, and yet is essential to life. Learning how to work with the energy that comes from the inner world belongs to the next stage in our evolution.

The first step is to use spiritual energy to break the patterns of collective identification that keep us imprisoned in a material view of life. These patterns have grown over the centuries, but in the past decades have become more invasive and powerful through the manipulation of corporations and the images of advertising. We are conditioned by a culture of consumerism and accumulation more than we know. The ideals of economic growth and prosperity are powerfully corruptive as they enshrine material well-being as the goal of the collective. This collective identification with material possessions creates a cloud over our consciousness that separates us from our spiritual nature. This identification needs to be broken. It has become too firmly cemented into our belief system to be gently removed. We are too addicted to our consumerism to be liberated except by a more powerful force. Such a force cannot be found in the outer world or any alternative pattern of belief.

The use of spiritual power in this arena is not without danger, as it would disturb a belief system that appears to give meaning to millions. Removing a protective covering, however imprisoning, can create unexpected vulnerability, fear, and anxiety. Moreover, such spiritual power would not impose any new belief system, but rather liberate individual consciousness from the cloud of a collective ideology. The need to free humanity from its addiction to material consumption is evident in the ecological crisis of the planet. This is one of the reasons that the intervention of a higher level of power is needed and allowed. At times of such extreme danger to the well-being of the whole, our spiritual guardians are allowed to participate directly in world affairs. This has not happened for many centuries, so we have forgotten even the possibility of such an intervention. We may allow for miracles to happen in our individual moments of crisis, but we rarely imagine that something similar can happen on a global level. Just as we have collectively forgotten that the world belongs to God, we have forgotten that "Thy will be done on earth as it is in heaven."

Miracles, like magic, are the intercession of a higher level of reality into a lower level. Something happens which does not belong to logic or the apparent laws of the situation. But when a higher reality interacts it follows the laws of its own level. For example, in the plane of oneness, which is the dimension of the Self, the limitations of time and space do not apply. Thus something can take place without any linear process of development. It just is. Our most common experience of this is intuition. We suddenly know something that we did not know a moment before—there is no process of deduction. Synchronicity is another example of a different level of reality interacting with our "normal" world, as seemingly chance occurrences have a meaning beyond our rational understanding. Our response to such situations is often an indication of how receptive we are to other dimensions within us. Do we even notice these moments when the inner world reveals itself? And if so, do we acknowledge and value their meaning, allowing our lives to be nourished and guided from within?

Such occurrences may lead us down previously un-explored pathways, open us to a wider perspective. What could be the effect of such occurrences on a collective level? Could they free the collective from its present patterns of identification? Or would they frighten it into clinging more tightly to what is familiar? If there is going to be a collective opening to a different level of reality, then there need to be those who are prepared for such an occurrence, so that the collective can be helped through a transition that might otherwise be too frightening. If the collective clutches too firmly at its familiar illusions, then an opportunity will be lost. But if it can be supported from within, then the whole of humanity can make the transition to a different level of consciousness. But what is fundamental is that this transition not be forced or coerced. Humanity is being offered a quality of freedom, not a new conditioning.

BREAKING PATTERNS OF WORLDLY POWER

The first step to allowing the collective access to a differ-ent level of consciousness is to break holes in its patterns of defense, in the dense clouds of materialistic thought-forms that dominate it. This is spiritual work that needs to be done carefully and with precision.

One might imagine that these holes would be made on the periphery of the collective power structure, where there is least resistance, maybe where alternative lifestyles meet with the energies of gross materialism. In the last decades many spiritual seekers have envisioned and to some degree created ideologies separate from the dominant material values, even formed groups and communities that embrace these alternative values. However, these are not the real places of power. Rather these are backwaters of the flow of the collective life force. They may uphold valuable spiritual, ecological, holistic values, but they do not fully interact with the life forces that now dominate the planet. Changes need to be made at the center of the places of worldly power, not at the edges. It is here that the real energy is waiting to be liberated.

The work is to break through at the core of our dominant power structures without those in positions of power being aware of the sabotage. The ancient way to accomplish this is to work from the inner planes where the patterns of power become constellated into thought-forms. Those who hold positions of power are so identified with the outer, material world that they are not even aware of the existence of the inner planes. Their focus is entirely outward, and so, "like a thief in the night," the energy of freedom can come unknown into their midst from within. How this is done is an esoteric secret, but it involves being inwardly present at places of power. One of the freedoms of those who have passed behind the veils of creation is that their presence is not limited by their physical bodies—through meditation and other practices they can be present wherever they are needed. The soul functions at a higher frequency than the physical world and like thought can be anywhere at any moment in time. This is how spiritual masters can teach their disciples without the need for physical nearness.

Although the soul can go where it is needed, it still experiences some difficulty in penetrating the dense clouds of material thought-forms. Their energy can be constricting, even suffocating, to a soul that is used to the fine light of spiritual aspiration. Also these places are covered with the darkness of corruption and misuse. Encountering the painful addictions of the world can be as disturbing on the inner planes as in physical life. But mystics go where they are needed without thought for themselves. The following dream describes such an experience:

> I was in the restroom of a main railway station. There were several rooms, very untidy and full of rubbish. There were hypodermic needles from drug addicts lying on the ground, excrement, and the definite smell of urine. Some people, especially women, lived there. I was horrified to see so much hardship. Suddenly I could see my teacher's leg through the door into another restroom. As I came to the other door we met each other. He was dressed completely in white and there was a very fine sense around him, the soft touch of something else. I was so glad and surprised to see him there. My joy was beyond measure. We hugged each other and he told me, "When we are told to be in such places, we are in such places."

The railway stations of the world are the places of our addictions, filled with refuse and excrement. The darkness and pain of our culture are very visible, in particular the pain caused by its treatment of women and the feminine. But mystics bring to such places the "soft touch of something else," an opening into the beyond.

The places of power in the world not only carry the darkness of their exploitation, but they also have at work in them forces that protect them. The cloying tentacles of greed can suck one's energy on the inner as well as the outer world. One can become lost in the multitude of illusions that swirl around these places, illusions that seem to belong to one's own hidden dreams and desires. These illusions constellate in the patterns of one's mind, may even seem helpful and beneficial, but are charged with a subtle self-interest. One needs to be very focused to penetrate these places and stay true to the purity of intention that drew one there.

Without a purity of intention and the protection of the friends of God it is best to avoid the places of worldly power. Their energy field magnifies our own weaknesses and patterns of self-deception. Even the desire to be helpful is a trap, and the longing to save the world a disaster. Spiritual poverty, "having nothing and wanting nothing," is our safeguard. But the darkness of these forces can also bring sadness, despair, and a longing to escape back to the light. Here are the soul-destroying, profit-hungry forces that drive our corporate culture. Here the inner wasteland of our material affluence is born. This is not a darkness that one can transform through devotion, but a power that needs to be penetrated.

Compassion may help to keep us from making judgments; love allow us to recognize that even this soul-destroying darkness belongs to God. But pure power is needed to break through these forces. And also laughter is needed—the inner laughter that knows this is part of the joke of our Beloved. The mystic knows that this is all an illusion, even though it brings despair to the soul. We know that only the touch of our Beloved is real, only the glance of His eyes has real substance. One needs a mystical sense of humor to encounter such darkness. If one took it too seriously there would be the danger of self-righteousness, of joining a crusade against the darkness. In these places where so many illusions are created and fostered, it is necessary to remember that even the darkness is not real.

WORKING WITH LIGHT

With focused intention and the power of our Beloved we can penetrate the places of worldly power from within. Then we need to hold a place of light in the darkness. This light will grow, and then a subtle change will take place. The light will reveal that the darkness is full of misplaced human hopes and dreams, full of misunderstanding and unhappiness. There is a deep sorrow in these places, like the pain in the drug addicts' restroom. Here is the collective sorrow of the soul. We need to work with this helpless despair, this longing for something other than material illusions. Our light can begin to change the substance of the darkness, to infuse hope into hopelessness. The power of our presence can reveal fundamental weaknesses in the logic of material thought-forms, their denial of humanity's prime purpose to praise God. We can bring the light of praise and remembrance into the darkness.

But the purpose of this work is not to dispel the darkness. That would take too long, and certain energies of darkness need to remain—they belong to the density of life. Our work is to have access to the power generating the illusions that govern our culture. There are specific places where this power is concentrated. Being present in these places of worldly power, we can infuse a seed of change, a potent catalyst that can constellate new thought-forms, generate new ideas. We can bring the energy of the coming era directly into the core of the places that generate worldly power. This is the only way that the next era can come into existence without the destruction of our present civilization.

In past eras a civilization that had become too corrupt and self-destructive was destroyed before a new era could be born. The destruction of the Roman Empire, brought about through its own self-indulgent weakness, created in its wake centuries of the Dark Ages in Europe. Only Noah and his ark escaped the great flood. Sometimes in our mythic past the destruction of a civilization was so absolute that it left few traces behind.

If we can change our present culture from within and alter the energy structure at its places of power, then we may be able to avoid the global catastrophe that our present exploitation is constellating. We have moved into a global era without realizing the consequences: a real catastrophe will no longer be local, no longer confined to a single geo-political area. Ecologically and economically we are living in a global arena where any imbalance affects the whole.

A web of light has been created around the world to contain the energy for this new evolution. The web around the world contains the higher energy, the new ideas that we need for our evolution. Through this web an energy is being given to humanity by the masters of wisdom, as a friend saw in a vision:

> In front of my inner eye I saw golden bodies of light in the form of balls and ellipses which were descending from above, out of the universe down to earth. There they partially dissolved, and nourished a golden web of light, which embraced the world. Other bodies of golden light went to specific places, especially towards the

top, the North Pole. They went through the web towards the center of the world in which there was an amphora of glistening white light, which rotated with tremendous speed. Around it sat many masters of wisdom in cheerfulness, joy, and happiness over an accomplished work. Every time new energy vibrated from the outside to the core of the heart it became stronger and faster and the gathering rejoiced quietly and laughed, some of them with tears in their eyes. I think I saw the Dalai Lama; he was laughing and deeply happy. There was an atmosphere of cheerfulness, relief, and seriousness at the same time, as after a successful experiment.

The rays of the heart of the world reached through the whole core of the world, but at this time don't yet reach its surface with their vibrations.

I had the feeling, or a brief glance, that these golden bodies of light came out of a huge funnel-shaped light-reservoir. They came in planned and particular rhythms and frequencies which reached the earth.

The web of light is a container for the new energy of life that is given from the higher planes by the masters of wisdom. The bodies of light nourish the whole world and are also directed at specific places, and in planned and particular rhythms. The masters carefully and joyfully direct this work, bringing the golden energy of light to the core of the heart of the world, whose light becomes stronger and vibrates faster.

However, the light from the core has not yet emerged to the surface. This is the next stage in the work. The web of light, created on the inner planes, needs now to be brought into the global power structure of the world. Then the energies of the inner and outer worlds can flow together. Together with global consciousness, the union of inner and outer is one of the cornerstones of the coming era. When the energy of this new era is linked with the economic and other power structures already present, there can be a dramatic shift, not just in global consciousness but also in the implementation of this consciousness. For example, the economic trading structures can be used for the benefit of the whole rather than for personal gain or exploitation. The way the internet has developed is an example of a new technology using an existing structure, the international phone system, to develop very quickly.

To access the places of worldly power, to connect the web of light with the worldly power structure and change its dynamics may seem just a dream. But a blueprint has been created for this work, an exact and detailed model of how this needs to be done. The first stage, creating a web of light, has taken place. The masters of wisdom are using this container to bring the energy where it is needed. Spiritual groups and individuals have also been inwardly aligned both with the web of light and with the power structure of the planet. But there needs to be a major breakthrough into the core places of power. This has not yet taken place. Part of the reason is the fragility of the worldly power structure. It is dangerously imbalanced and the friends of God are working to prevent the whole system from falling apart.

The work of the friends of God has always been hidden, taking place in the inner realms. Part of the demand of the present is that this work become visible to some degree; part of their work needs to be known. Humanity can no longer afford to be ignorant of its spiritual nature or of the spiritual potential of the planet. A certain knowledge needs to be given to humanity about the real purpose of life and the evolution of the planet. But when a work that has begun on the inner planes begins to break through into outer life, there is a danger, just as the birth of a child is more dangerous than the time of pregnancy. In the inner there are coverings of protection that do not exist in the outer world.

The outer global energy structure and its dynamics of power are neither balanced nor stable. Into this structure a new, more powerful energy of change needs to be infused, and part of this process involves making the inner visible in the outer. This work cannot be forced, and yet it needs to happen within a certain time frame, before the clouds of greed and exploitation cover the light of the planet in a way that is irreversible. In service to what is real, we pray for help in this work. In the final picture of his vision, my friend saw himself in the Kalyan mosque, the main mosque at Bukhara (the ancient center of the *Khwâjagân*). "I was prostrating myself desperately until my knees were bleeding, so that His mercy may be greater than His wrath. I asked for true modesty and humility so that humans, we humans, could be together with Him again."

THE POWER OF THE REAL

Listen, O dearly beloved!
I am the reality of the world,
the center of the circumference,
I am the parts and the whole.
I am the will established between Heaven and Earth.

Ibn 'Arabî[1]

THE ENACTMENT OF DIVINE WILL

Worldly power is ultimately an illusion, often originating in the ego's fantasies of its omnipotence. In our adversarial culture, power is also usually understood in terms of dominance over others. One person or group has the power to make others do what they want, forcing another's body, even his mind, to do their bidding, to follow their will. Frequently fear is involved; through fear the lesser is forced to accede to the will of the greater. Occasionally worldly powers are confronted by individuals, like Gandhi and Nelson Mandela, whose power and freedom come from a deeper source and reveal the underlying frailty of our common understanding of power. But collectively we accept the dictates of power, even when we may rebel against them.

The power of the Real is unlike worldly power, and also unlike many lower forms of spiritual power. Real power belongs to That which is omnipotent and is an expression of absolute omnipotence. Its nature is not adversarial, except when it involves the mastery of the ego or lower nature, the *nafs*. Sometimes a lesser form of spiritual power may be misused to have influence over others; this happens when the mastery of the ego has not been accomplished.

The power of the Real is an enactment of divine will. In order for His will to be enacted there needs to be an energy to make it happen. But on the highest level His will and the power to bring it into being are not separate, just as there is no separation between the intention and the act. It is.

This level of power and divine will can only be enacted by one who is merged with the divine, who is in a state of oneness. The friends of God are one with their Beloved, and yet also appear in a state of separation while in this world. Traditionally, the state of servant-hood comes after the stage of union with God. Merged in God, His servants are authorized to enact His will, although in truth there is not the duality of servant and master. The working of His will through His servant is described in a sixteenth-century history of the *Khwâjagân*, in an explanation of the statement, "Whatever he says, Allâh will do":

> The deep meaning of this statement is that no will remains within the servant and everything consists of manifestation of Divine Will. As a matter of fact, Allâh has such servants as have extinguished their own will in the Will of Allâh, acquired the at-tributes of extinction and perpetuity, and attained to the degree of genuine incapacity and poverty, servitude and loyal obedience. As for the heart that stays at this degree, it is like a page exposed to Allâh's pen. Nothing contrary to Allâh's will can therefore be willed, so their wish is always that which Allâh wishes.... Such people are those who are learned in esoteric knowledge and protected from the disasters of the lower self.[2]

If we are to understand the nature of divine power, we have to leave behind the hierarchical image of power structures to which we have become accustomed. When we recognize a brotherhood of spiritual masters enacting the will of God in the visible and invisible worlds, we are taken into a spiritual environment that is less static and easily defined, in which different levels of reality can merge together in service to the One.

In this more fluid model there is no above or below, but a dynamic, interdependent whole in which we encounter the unmanifest and manifest aspects of the divine interacting together, with human and divine will playing their parts. The friends of God enact His will; their will is His will. There are other invisible forces that help to determine our existence, and yet we also determine our own existence. We have been given free will, but as the whole of humanity belongs to God, we are also subservient to divine will—not, however, in the simple formula of ruler and ruled, because that suggests duality and the divine wholeness is one.

The intercession of divine will often comes as a direct response to human need. Human and divine work together. The idea that God has plans for us is too child-like. Rather we are the enactment of a divine idea, and this divine idea also gives us free will. Humanity and the planet have the potential to develop in certain ways, and also the freedom to choose their level and pattern of development. The work of the friends of God is to make accessible to humanity the greatest possible freedom of choice, to remind humanity of the degrees of development that are possible. And yet in the unfolding of oneness, no way is better or worse.

A NEW LEVEL OF AWARENESS

Humanity can become free from its self-destructive focus on the material plane and aware of other nonphysical levels of existence. Human beings are not merely physical creatures, but have access to other levels of reality. These other levels are traditionally accessible by the individual through spiritual practices. However, there is also the possibility at certain times for humanity as a whole to be given access to a different level of awareness. This is the opportunity of the present time, and it is the work of His friends to give humanity this choice: to stop humanity from closing this door.

Our present collective focus is very intent upon the material plane, more so than in previous cultures that had a spiritual focus at their core. Our material fixation has created a web of illusory images that bind our attention to this plane. We believe in the myths of materialism, the supposed happiness that can come from the consumption of material goods. What we do not realize is how strongly this addiction blinds us to another reality that is around us. Sadly, many of the traditional methods of opening our eyes, religions and spiritual paths, are caught in their own hierarchical power structures and have lost touch with our essential freedom. These power structures are very resistant to real change, as that would involve their dissolution.

But if we relate to life as a living organism which functions on many different levels and is an expression of the divine, we see that change is a necessary part of our evolution. Without change and adaptation to a changing environment any organism dies. We have substantially changed our environment, particularly since the industrial revolution. We have even changed our climate patterns.

It is only natural that humanity itself should adapt and change. Logically we know that we cannot continue our gluttony of consumption, but our ability to recognize the possibility for real change appears limited. Collectively we still see change within the material paradigm that has created the present situation. Yet any successful organism opens up new possibilities for growth at such a time. Evolving through accessing a different level of consciousness is a simple response to our present predicament. Initially all that is required is to make the collective aware of such a possibility.

How can one make humanity see beyond the material spectrum? One solution is to open doorways of light into the present spectrum of consciousness. These doorways need to open directly into the material consciousness of the present. Humanity is so blinkered in its focus, so addicted to materialism, that it is not enough to say, "Over there is a new way of living that is free." Humanity cannot turn its attention away from its present fixation. The other world needs to be made visible directly into this world. For this the use of divine power is necessary in order to break through the coverings of the physical world and its patterns of illusion that dominate our collective consciousness.

However, the dimensions of light upon light can be very disturbing to someone used to living in the shadowy landscape of our present awareness. This is one reason why the friends of God have kept their work secret over the centuries. Normally the light, love, and wisdom of the inner realms are carefully filtered down to ordinary life, appearing as minor miracles, sudden insights, or other acceptable, if not fully understandable, happenings. The impact of the Real upon our world of carefully constructed illusions can be undermining and destabilizing.

There could be a severe shock to a collective so identified with a material reality.

Any individual who has experienced a transition to a different level of awareness knows how destabilizing it can be. Patterns of identity, notions of self, are swept away or dissolved. So are patterns of control. One's relationship to oneself, to others, and to the outer world are changed by forces that are not yet fully integrated. There can be both unexpected joy and unexpected sadness as deep feelings are released. Part of spiritual training is learning to live with such changes, to go with the flow that comes from within and always brings the unexpected. In many instances the only form of preparation is to know that one cannot be prepared. Yet there is a deep wonder as the horizon expands, as a previous sense of self gives way to a new and richer perspective on life and the divine.

In order to make these transitions we often need to know that others have gone before us, that even if we are stepping into an unknown inner landscape there are footsteps to follow. Sometimes a guide or spiritual teacher is needed to contain us, particularly when we go through experiences of dissolution when our whole sense of self falls away and we remain in a state of extreme insecurity and vulnerability. Gradually a new state of consciousness constellates and we learn how to function in a different way. Without a guide or teacher the insecurity might be too intense and the new level of awareness might not constellate.

If humanity is to make a transition to a new level of awareness, it needs to know that it is guided, and that this transition is not a chance occurrence but a shift that has long been planned. This is one of the reasons that the inner needs to become visible, that the masters of wisdom may become known. Humanity is mainly guided from the inner world, but at certain times this invisible guidance is not enough. One can witness how great souls like Gandhi and Nelson Mandela helped their countries through a difficult time of transition with a minimum of bloodshed. The masters of wisdom do not need to take the role of worldly leaders but they may need to make known to humanity some of the care, love, and wisdom with which we are all guided and supported. A certain knowledge has to be given to humanity for it to make this transition, and this knowledge cannot be given entirely in the inner world. There needs to be a collective conscious recognition of the power of the divine.

FOCUSING DIVINE ENERGY

The energy of the divine is everywhere. All life is supported by this primal power. Without the energy of the divine there would be no existence—it is the sunlight upon which everything depends. The energy of the divine flows from the inner, uncreated worlds into the world of manifestation, but for the most part it is diffuse, unfocused. Like sunlight it falls everywhere, nourishing all forms of life. Traditionally part of the work of the friends of God has been to focus this light where it is needed, to be like a lens that focuses the sunlight in a particular place.

Existing outside of space and time, and yet also present in this world, these masters reflect the light from the inner to the outer planes, ensuring that the correct amount of light comes to a particular place or person. On an individual level this is how they work with their disciples, giving each wayfarer the specific amount of light, love, power that is needed for their development.

Too much light and the individual would be blinded, unbalanced. Too little light and her potential for transformation would be limited.

Some traditions also work with spiritual groups in this way, giving the energy of the divine to the group as a whole. As with an individual, the amount of divine energy that is given to a group must be carefully monitored. For example, if a group is too focused on its own dynamics, too inward-looking, then a certain energy is withheld. A spiritual group—like an individual wayfarer—must be gradually awakened to the dimensions of servanthood. In this process each individual contributes to the dynamic of the whole group, and yet the group also has a life of its own. In the Sufi tradition the *sheikh* watches over the group like his own family, giving it the energy it needs for its development and work. On the outer plane this energy can be given through group meetings; on the inner plane it is done through the inner connection from heart to heart and the merging of souls.

A spiritual group is a container for inner work, providing a place of protection and nourishment for the individual wayfarer. Being in the company of friends is of great assistance on the path. To quote Rûmî:

> Every prophet sought out companions.
> A wall standing alone is useless,
> but put three or four walls together,
> and they'll support a roof and keep
> the grain dry and safe.[3]

A spiritual group is also involved in the work of service. The energy given to a group makes the group spin at a particular frequency, and it is through the spinning hearts of the lovers of God that certain spiritual work is done in the inner and outer worlds. A group that spins with light and love at a particular frequency is a powerful spiritual organism. Through this spinning a certain darkness in the world can be transmuted, a certain pollution cleansed. The spinning of love and light can also awaken people to their own divinity. The spiritual master or *sheikh* can also use the group as a way of focusing divine power into energy centers in the world, in the same way that an individual disciple is used to bring light and love to a particular place or person.

Moreover, a group can work directly with the collective in a way that is difficult for an individual. The energy of the group counterbalances the pull of the collective and it can go to the core of the collective without being overwhelmed. The collective is a powerful force, a body of thought-forms, desires, impulses that pulls individuals into its patterns. It is easy to get sucked into the energy field of the collective where real individuality is lost. The force field of a spiritual group protects the wayfarer from this danger, and enables the group to interact directly with the energy dynamic of the collective.

Also, because a group is not caught in the limitations and boundaries of a single individual's identity, the group's energy can flow more easily in and out of the energy patterns of the collective. At present a certain spiritual work needs to be done directly with the collective and its energy structure. A spiritual group can focus a stream of energy into the core of the collective, helping to change certain energy patterns.

How can a small group of mystics alter the energy structure of many thousands, even millions of people? Both on the inner and outer planes, a group can bring the more fluid and potent energy of the inner world into the collective. It can bring the light of remembrance into the darkness of our collective forgetfulness. And a group held within the heart of a *sheikh* who is merged with the Absolute can bring the power of the Absolute directly into the core of the collective. The power of the Absolute enacts the will of God, and thus can change anything in the created and uncreated worlds.

Working from the inner planes, a group can remain mainly invisible, but the enactment of the power of the Real could still break apart many of the illusions that contain our collective view of life. This power is like the sword of Allâh, cutting away the illusions that separate us from our true nature. It does not always respect the delicate diplomacy of our ego dynamics.

To enact the power of the Real requires a master who has been trained in its use. The danger is always that it could free us from too many illusions, so that we would burn in the bright sunlight of Truth. On the individual journey there comes a time when this is necessary, when we have to die to all of the illusions that give substance to the ego. But this level of initiation is not appropriate for the collective. That is why the power of the Real usually remains veiled when it is used. But the illusions that presently cover us and suck our lifeblood cling so tightly that the sword of the Real may need to act unveiled in order to free us and give us access to the light of our true nature.

It is important to recognize that such power cannot be compared to any form of worldly power, or even many lower forms of spiritual power. The power of the Real is never used for dominance. Its quality of light is too bright to allow for corruption or misuse. And it always recognizes the uniqueness and integrity of everyone, because this is the stamp of the Creator. Something in the individual bows down before this power, because in our deepest self we are all in service to God; we are all here to witness that He is Lord.

But how can we reconcile individual freedom with such an overwhelming power? In our world we have few images of a power that does not dominate. We have even projected the dynamics of domination onto nature, and in response attempt to subdue its forces. But if we can move beyond images of duality, we can acknowledge that a higher power can liberate through the energy of freedom rather than domination. This was enacted in the breakdown of communism and the fall of the Berlin Wall in 1989. The people of Eastern Europe expressed their desire for freedom, and the forces of oppression dissolved. There was no massive bloodshed or liberating army. Something was awakened within the people which freed them. It seemed like a miracle.

THE FOUNDATIONS OF THE NEW ERA

Our present collective patterns of control do not want a miracle to take place, as that would lessen their power. They are happy that the "spiritual" remains in the arena of the individual—is an alternative lifestyle, or, on a more collective level, concerns itself with good works and social welfare. Worldly power then remains in the hands of politicians, generals, and executives. What would happen to these "leaders" if the power of the Real became visible? How would they react? Could they even recognize a power that does not act through control, that does not even oppose their power but functions in a totally different way?

The Real dissolves or destroys illusions, rouses us from our sleep of forgetfulness. The journey of the in-dividual soul begins when the glance of the Beloved, the light of the Real, awakens us for an instant. That momentary glimpse is what inspires and calls us to make the journey home. The simple presence of the Real cuts through the illusions that define our world and opens us to a different way of being. How would this same energy affect the collective?

Without the power of the Real we will be starved of a new energy we need. We will become more and more suffocated by the illusions we have created. What we do not fully appreciate is how these illusions pollute us on the inner as well as the outer plane. It is not just our planet but also our soul that is being desecrated. The lifeblood of real meaning is being denied us. The degree of our collective forgetfulness means that we are dying to the true purpose of our existence. Only the Real can fully penetrate this dark cloud of forgetfulness, awaken us, bring the spark of remembrance back to the whole of humanity. The Real speaks with the voice of God, acts with His will. And the Real is our own deepest essence, the substance of our being. Its energy is all around us, but unfocused. The work of the friends of God is simply to focus and direct this energy to where it is needed.

If we are to create a new civilization, then we need the power of the Real not only to break up the old patterns, but to lay the foundations for what is to come. At the beginning of every era a spark is given to humanity to help it to evolve, and with this spark is given the energy needed for this unfolding. The spark of the next era is already present: it has a quality of love and unity that expresses itself as global awareness and a deepening care and responsibility for the whole of life and the planet. But the tendency of humanity is to create an illusion of whatever is given, to weave what is new into the fabric of our desires and conditioning. This can be seen in the individual journey of the wayfarer when the initial spark of revelation becomes lost in a web of spiritual desires and other ego dynamics. The simplicity and wonder of what is given become buried under personal patterns, ambition, problems, emotional needs. A teacher is often necessary to point the wayfarer back to what is essential, the inner call of the soul for Truth. And an unconditioned energy that is free of these patterns is needed to take us along the way. Without the power of the path we could not take a single step.

This is also true of the collective. The spark of the "new age" that arrived unexpectedly with the coming of Eastern spiritual traditions to the West has already been marketed in many forms from self-development to methods of psychic awakening. It has become a part of our buying and selling and developed power structures to foster its expansion. A certain simplicity and wonder have almost been lost. The power of the Real will take us back to what is essential and enable the true qualities of the coming era to be grounded in everyday life. Energy is needed to create foundations that have real substance, that are not just spiritual fantasies. The inner container for the work has been formed, but a different energy is now needed to bring the new into the density of our physical existence.

The foundations of the new era have to belong to life itself, not some image of life. At the core of all existence is the call to praise Him and serve Him. This is the primal song of every cell and it belongs to the depths of our instinctual nature. This call to praise has been forgotten, covered over with all the illusions of life that we have created over the centuries. We have created a fabric of life based upon our desires rather than upon His call. We need to return to what is fundamental to life, to create our foundation upon His imprint, upon what is real. And we must be aware of the danger of creating a spiritual illusion in place of our present material illusions. Much of the initial energy of this new era has created spiritual illusions that are an escape from life rather than a full engagement in life. But if we do not fully engage in life from the spiritual core of our being, life will die. Life needs us to recognize its oneness, how His name is imprinted in all of creation.

The power of the Real belongs to all of life and cannot create a spiritual illusion. The energy of the Real speaks to the very cells of creation, recognizing His imprint. The Real can strip away the illusions that cover and suffocate not only ourself but life itself. It can enable life to breathe and sing again, to praise and remember Him. Life will respond to this power just as our hearts respond to the energy of That which we truly love. We have denied the world its divinity; now we are needed to help reawaken it, to be present in the midst of life and allow the power of His presence to live within us, to be true to what is real. Without our participation, the energy of the Real cannot fully penetrate life. Humanity is a cocreator of life and the energy of life follows the patterns of our consciousness.

Prana, the energy of life, follows thought. With every breath the energy of life flows from the inner to the outer, and our consciousness directs its flow. This is one of the reasons why the practice of the *dhikr* or *mantra* which is done with the breath is so important, not just to the individual but to the whole of life. Repeating His name with the breath, we consciously align the energy of life with the Creator, with the highest principle. This simple practice nourishes life on many different levels.

On the level of the collective our addiction to materialism, the way greed and the thoughts of accumulation govern our consciousness, means that the energy of life is polluted by these thoughts before it even comes fully into existence. Collectively we deny life a certain spiritual nourishment and instead pollute it with our thoughts, which often involve the desecration and exploitation of life itself. Our thoughts as well as our actions exploit the world for our own consumption. We take rather than give to life and have the collective arrogance to believe that we should have what we want. Our corporations foster these beliefs, becoming successful, wealthy, and powerful by both creating and fulfilling our desires.

Through our inner alignment we can bring the energy of the Real into the fabric of life where it can break up these patterns and return life to what is real. Life can then respond. When we give the energy of the Real to life, the real purpose of life can awaken, can breathe and sing. And then we can recognize what it means to be a human being, what it means to be alive. This is part of the promise of the future.

To embrace the energy of the Real means to step outside of the collective and participate directly in life as it is. What does this mean? For each of us it will be different because we are each a unique expression of His love. There are no rules because we have not yet lived this dimension of ourselves. There is no pattern to follow because every moment has its own singular beauty and magic. But something is calling us to fully engage with life. Not to conceal ourself in its illusions—material or spiritual—but to embrace life as a direct expression of our Beloved. For the Sufi the simple practice of remembrance returns us to the pure source of our being and the unpolluted energy of life. Remembering our Beloved with each and every breath, we bring His energy into the world, reminding every cell of creation to whom it belongs. The power of remembrance comes from the direct connection between lover and Beloved, the conscious affirmation of "He loves them and they love Him."

In the oneness of His love everything is included. Living the remembrance of God, we affirm this oneness with joy and commitment. We give to the whole the purest energy of life, an energy that comes from the inner worlds stamped with the recognition of His name. When we walk in the shadows of this world, we see its many problems. But in the pure light we will be shown the ways of healing and transformation that belong not just to ourselves but to the whole planet. These ways are waiting to be revealed, but they need the light of the Real to become visible. They need our commitment to witness Him in His world.

The foundations of the next era need to be made from what is real, not from an illusion. Only our relationship to God is real, our innermost need to praise and witness Him. This relationship is not born in this world of illusion, but belongs to the soul. It is the spark in the heart that is in every child, but so easily becomes covered over by the illusions of the world. Mystics are those who live this innermost relationship without care for the consequences: they belong to Him since before they were born. They have the responsibility to lay the foundations for the next age, to bring the stamp of His presence into the consciousness of the world. For this they need a certain power to break through the patterns of resistance that would deny any real change. And the world needs His imprint impressed back into the consciousness of humanity, which has forgotten Him.

Divine consciousness can reflect the light of higher frequencies and also hold the energy of darkness in a way that does not distort our perception. Reflecting higher frequencies of light into this world will nourish humanity in ways we cannot imagine. Containing the darkness will stabilize our culture, protecting it from the danger of too much light, of expanding too fast. Darkness and light belong together in a dynamic not of conflict but of cooperation. Within humanity darkness and light are needed to balance each other. Remembrance also recognizes our role as His servant and so limits the danger of hubris which causes our fall from grace.

Divine consciousness spins at a frequency that purifies its environment. It can keep humanity protected from certain power dynamics and patterns of greed. And it has within it the laughter that belongs to the core of life, the laughter of a revelation that is always changing and always misunderstood. Sometimes we catch this laughter, even in the midst of life's suffering and challenges. We know for an instant that life is more than we can comprehend, that behind its appearance another reality is speaking to us in riddles.

THE LIGHT OF THE SOUL

His light may be compared to a niche
wherein is a lamp
the lamp in a glass,
the glass as it were a glittering star
kindled from a Blessed Tree,
an olive that is neither of the East nor of the West
whose oil would almost shine forth
though no fire touches it
Light upon Light
Allah guides to His Light whom He will.

Qur'an 24:35

WORKING WITH THE SOUL OF THE WORLD

Our souls are made of a quality of light, a light that belongs to God and carries a knowing of its source. Through this light the soul sees its way, the path it follows, the destiny that needs to be lived. Without this light there could be no evolution, no meaning to life.

Spiritual life is a means to bring the light of the soul into the world. Spiritual practices give us access to our light and the teachings of the path help us live it in our daily life. The more our light shines in this world, the easier it is to follow a spiritual path and be guided from within. Through this light the inner meaning of the soul comes into our life, and the wonder of God becomes visible. In this light we see the oneness that belongs to God, that is a direct expression of His nature. Without it we only see the reflections of our illusory self, the shadows of the ego.

The world also has a soul. The world is a living be-ing, of which an individual human being is a microcosm. The soul of the world is the spiritual heart of the world, a spinning organism of light and love that exists at its core. Without this light the world would fade away; it would be just shadowy images without purpose or meaning. The light of our own soul brings meaning to our lives, and turning away from the needs of our soul brings dark-ness and despair. Similarly, the soul of the world makes the world sacred, and our mistreatment of the world is a desecration.

The light of the soul of the world is everywhere. Just as the soul of the individual is present throughout the body, the soul of the world permeates every cell of creation. Because we can access the soul of the world through our own higher nature, we can access it wherever we are, in any situation. And there are specific ways to work with it, to bring its quality of light into life. There are ways for its light to interact with the darkness of the world and transform the darkness, to reveal hidden qualities within humanity. And there are also ways to help its light flow around the world. When the light of the soul flows around the world, it can open and activate energy centers in the energy structure of the planet, energy centers that are needed for the next level of human evolution, which is also the evolution of our planet.

On one level the light of the soul of the world *is* the light of humanity, both individually and collectively. It is made up of the light of the souls of all of humanity and a substance that belongs to the very being of the planet. It comes into existence through us and through the physical body of the planet. But it does not belong to the physical dimension. It is fully alive in a different dimension where its light is clearly visible. In this dimension it can interact with other similar bodies of light, other celestial energies that are invisible to us. And the soul of the world is itself part of a vast living organism, a pulsating body of light we call the Milky Way.

In the inner worlds, the light of the soul is guided by the masters of love; in the outer world it needs our attention. The contribution of the mystic is to be open to the inner energy structure of life, to the light of the soul of the world. We can learn to work directly with this light, to become a conscious node in its organic web. Then our higher consciousness can directly participate with the light of the whole—we will no longer be isolated within our individual aspiration, but can make a direct contribution to the way the light moves around the planet.

Every human being can participate in this unfolding. This light is not other than us, and yet it needs to live through us. It comes into life through the core of our being, where we are directly connected to the divine. We need to bring this energy into the outer flow of life, into the places of darkness and the shadows of misunderstanding. Once we step out of the sphere of self-interest into a real concern with the whole, we have access to the energy of the whole. We are open to the light of the world and can use it. Without the light of the soul of the world to guide us, life cannot fulfill its larger purpose; its real destiny cannot unfold.

But there are many forces in the world that deny the world its light. On an individual level the darkness of our own greed or selfishness inhibits the flow of our own light into life. Similarly, our collective darkness covers the world with patterns of greed and desire for power. These are the forces whose stories we read in our newspapers, whose ambitions cause suffering. This darkness is visible all around us. With global news coverage we see how it creates suffering around the world. We see the hungry and destitute and the damage of war. We know the pollution caused by corporations and read stories of their corruption and greed. We recognize how the politics of power care only for more power and wealth, rarely for the well-being of the whole.

What we do not see so clearly is how the light of the soul of the world works, how its energy flows through the hearts of individuals, how it brings hope where there is despair, joy into the midst of suffering. Our eyes are so attuned to the darkness that we miss light's power and beauty. But we can begin to recognize the ways light flows through the world, and learn to work with it. We need to guide the light of the soul of the world into the centers of worldly power. This light needs to show the whole world the way, bring meaning back to the mass of humanity.

Bringing the light of the soul of the world into the collective consciousness of humanity requires perseverance and patience. There are forces of self-interest that resist the light. There are patterns of control that can only exist in the darkness or the shadows, and these do not want the light to affect them. They are often constellated around fears or desires that are based upon illusions. When the illusions are revealed, they lose their control. In the bright light of the divine many forces of darkness lose their power or simply dissolve.

We know how this happens in our own journey: how the light gained through aspiration and given by grace helps us to see the patterns that constrict us, the darkness that binds us. Seeing these patterns with the clear light of consciousness can often cause them to lose their power so that they no longer dominate us. Working with the light of the world can have a similar effect on collective patterns. First one has to break through the resistance to real light—not the reflected light of the ego and the mind, but the pure light of the soul. Then one has to move the light around, so that it can flow with the energy of life, follow the riverbeds of creation. In this way it can nourish the whole of humanity and bring meaning back into the deserts we have created.

Part of the wonder of the energy of the soul is its quality of oneness. In this oneness the energy and the knowledge of how it works are one. In each moment oneness reveals to us how to work with it: how to guide its flow and how to overcome or work around the obstacles that impede it. What is required of the servant is an openness of heart and purity of intention. If we want something for ourself, we cannot have access to the light or learn how to work with it. If we are in service to the whole, we are given what we need to help with the work.

How do we begin this work? In order to work with the light we must accept the darkness, for in His oneness everything is included. We must recognize that darkness—greed, suffering, selfishness—is also a part of our world. The darkness is part of our nature, part of our heritage. We are the fallen angel and this world is our home.

Light and darkness appear to be simple opposites. Like any opposites they can be in conflict with each other or come together in a way that is creative. Our scriptures speak of the battles of light and darkness, good and evil. But our psychology tells a different story, of light hidden in the depths of darkness, and how darkness can be transformed, lead turned into gold.

The time of polarizing light and dark is over. It was a dynamic of the past era of duality. For hundreds of years we have lived within the paradigm of duality, of opposites that are in continual conflict. This was the era of the warring brothers in which the primal forces of life appeared in opposition. So many battles have been fought, so much blood spilled. Another paradigm is now constellating; another era has begun. In this new paradigm the opposites can come together in a new way. We can work with the light of the soul of the world and the darkness of the world in a creative relationship.

BEYOND THE OPPOSITES OF DARKNESS AND LIGHT

How can light and darkness dance together? How can we work with the soul of the world in the density and confusion of everyday life? How can we bring this light into the places of worldly power and help it guide the destiny of nations?

Since the individual is a microcosm of the whole, we can use the model of working with the light of our own soul to understand how to work with the light of the soul of the world.

The light of the soul is not a foreign substance. It is a part of our own nature, but usually remains hidden beneath the coverings of our lower self. Our darkness hides us from our light. But what many don't understand is that the darkness is also needed to engage the light, just as suffering often lifts our face towards God. We may think that our suffering and the divine are opposites, that God is goodness and light while our suffering comes from the darkness. But this duality is essentially an illusion. Suffering is an aspect of life energy being restricted by matter, being caught in its darkness. Often suffering comes from resistance to change, and change is fundamental to life. Even the miracle of birth brings the pain of childbirth. Energy and matter work together; for example, our breath follows the deeper rhythms of life, which is why conscious breathing can lessen our pain and help us go with the flow of life.

There is a flow of life that belongs to the miracle of creation, and the darkness is part of this miracle. Accepting our darkness, accepting the suffering of life, we are taken into the crucible of transformation in which the opposites come together. A deeper oneness is revealed, not as an ideal but as a lived reality. Knowing this oneness, we can participate in life in a new way, no longer thrown between the opposites but recognizing and working with life's deeper patterns, its underlying energy. This is a part of the initiation of the mystic and the shaman, whose journey through suffering gives them access to life's hidden powers. Traditionally such a journey has allowed them to work with the energy of the soul of the world. They know the meaning of the darkness and the purity of light, and how they can come together for individual and collective healing and transformation.

One can only have access to the light of the soul if one lives in the present, accepting what is. At this time in history, this means to accept a certain degree of darkness that is present. One of the reasons that in the West we have so little access to this light is that we are conditioned not to live in the present. We are either chasing our desires or trying to escape our fears. We are rarely content with what is. A Pueblo Indian described this quality of the white man in talking to Carl Jung, "Their eyes have a staring expression; they are always seeking something. What are they seeking? The whites always want something; they are always uneasy and restless."[1]

We are conditioned to pursue an illusive happiness, while being bombarded by the media with images that manipulate us into continual dissatisfaction and desires.

The simplicity of living in the present moment has become a spiritual ideal rather than an ordinary reality. If we are to reclaim our heritage of light, we first have to reclaim the present moment. This means to accept the combination of light and darkness as it is. Only then can we work towards a better future.

It may sound contradictory that in order to work for a better future for humanity we have to accept life as it is, but a real future is built upon the present. Only in the present moment can we have access to the energies that can heal and transform us. Living in the past and future, we are caught in our fantasies. In the present we are open to the light of the divine.

In each moment as we watch the breath, we see how energy flows from the inner to the outer, and we consciously participate in this cycle of creation. Being present in our own lives is the doorway to participating in the miracle of divine revelation. The soul of the world needs to be born in every moment, to participate in the constantly changing creation. "God is upon some new task daily." Through simple awareness we connect the higher with the lower, the inner plane of pure awareness with the outer world of events, and our own consciousness with the consciousness of the whole.

When we are fully present in the midst of life, we connect the worlds together, and through this connection the light can flow. We are the gateways for love and light to pour into the world and awaken the world to its own sacredness. Just as *prana*, or life energy, follows thought, the light of the soul of the world is guided by our attitude and attention. It follows the orientation of our heart, the way we participate in life from our depths. The more we are oriented towards what is real within ourselves and our own lives, the more easily the Real can flow into the world.

FIGHTING THE FORCES OF FORGETFULNESS

Light is present everywhere, yet hidden and unused. It is covered over by the denseness of our desires and a collective consciousness that has little space for the divine. Working with the light of the soul will open us to a new level of interconnectedness, a *knowing* of oneness. This knowing is necessary for the evolution of the planet. It contains the knowledge of the future, a knowledge that is based upon oneness rather than duality.

An awareness of global oneness has begun to constellate. The idea of the unity of life, that "we are one," no longer belongs just to a spiritual or ecological fringe, yet is becoming part of the mainstream. But this awareness is lacking an essential ingredient—it is still an idea, it is not fully alive. When it becomes alive, the heart of the world will open and we will hear its song, the song of the oneness of life. The unity of life is a direct expression of the divine and it is our lived connection to the divine that gives us meaning. This song will remind us of our true nature and why we are here.

This is like the process of our own awakening. Over many years we might be given glimpses of our true nature, the wisdom and love within us. We work to purify ourselves, to contribute in service to life and love. And one day something comes alive within us. Our heart awakens, and we experience a greater power and knowing beyond ourselves. This is the potential of the moment in the world. Our world's soul can awaken, and all humanity can come to know its true nature.

The world has to awaken from its sleep of forgetfulness—it can no longer afford to forget its divinity. More than any pollution, it is this forgetfulness that is killing the earth. The awakening of the soul of the world can redeem what has been desecrated, heal what has been wounded, purify what has been polluted. Collectively we are dying—we have forgotten our purpose, and a life-form that has forgotten its purpose cannot survive. Its fundamental reason for existence fades away. The awakening of the soul of the world will remind us all why we are here and the whole of life will rejoice.

Forgetfulness is not just an absence of remembrance. The cloud of forgetfulness that covers so much of our world is not just an absence of light. Our forgetfulness of our divine purpose is like a sticky substance that draws life into its web, where it devours any meaning life may have. This cloud is not just the *maya* of illusion but a density that ensures that we remain slaves to our lower nature. Our collective forgetfulness will stop us from hearing the song of the world and deny us our future.

There is much work to be done to prepare the world stage for this awakening; otherwise the dawn will come unnoticed, and once again humanity will have missed an opportunity. We have to bring the light of oneness to the places of forgetfulness. We have to create a network of light within the planes of creation. This network is a container for the awakening of the heart of the world so that the meaning of this event can become known, so that we can hear its song.

But the potency of forgetfulness is such that we have to force open some of the gateways of light. We have to drag the light down into life and fight with the darkness. Once again the battle of light and darkness has to be fought, and once again the darkness has disguised itself in the forms of worldly success. This could be the last real battle at the end of the era of opposites, and much of it is hidden, fought by individuals who dare to lift their faces to the light. Our remembrance of what is real, of the divine that is the essence of life, is countering the forces of forgetfulness and their dynamics of worldly power and corruption. And as always, what happens on the outer stage is a distorted reflection of the real drama of the soul.

When the oneness of life becomes fully alive, it will activate energy centers in life that belong only to oneness, that cannot be accessed through the consciousness of duality. The energy of oneness can link us together; the light of the soul of the world can give us access to these places of inner power that are needed to overturn the entrenched positions of worldly power. This is a work that we are doing individually and together.

There is an urgency to this work, to free the world of certain patterns before the heart of the world opens. And we have to be prepared to fight for what we believe, to commit ourselves to the light of the soul and the awakening of the ways of oneness. This may seem like a spiritual ideal, but anyone who has confronted the darkness of the world knows the intensity and demands of this fight. Unfortunately this work cannot be done just through love and acceptance. Just as there are forces in our own psyche that must be confronted and disarmed before they can be integrated,[2] so are there forces in the world that will not respond to compassion or kindness, but must be confronted with a sword of light.

The potency of spiritual light must be brought into the marketplace of life. In this light we can see things as they really are and so disarm the forces of darkness. The forces of darkness need subterfuge and deception to win us over. Spiritual light will strip them of these coverings and reveal their true nature; we will see how the forces of greed corrupt us, how they deny us our freedom and joy, and how the ideology of consumerism is a plague that sucks the nourishment away from life. But first we have to confront these forces, and although we have to do this individually we cannot do it alone. They are too powerful.

Part of the wonder of the ways of oneness is that we are linked together through our unique individual nature. When we make connections through oneness, we will discover how we support each other in ways that enhance our individual contribution. The ways of oneness give us freedom rather than codependency. And the ways of oneness move faster than the forces of the world. They belong to the next era of our evolution and spin at a higher frequency. If we can connect together through the ways of oneness, the forces of darkness can be stripped of their power. These forces do not need to be destroyed, only disarmed. Then they can be transformed, their darkness integrated into the whole.

CONFRONTING THE COLLECTIVE DARKNESS

Stepping firmly into the darkness of the world, we will confront many of the sins of our fathers, the depths of our collective desecration, pain caused by patriarchal power drives, and the repression and abuse of the feminine. Joy has been stripped from life and our spiritual nature abused and corrupted. Just as our individual journey confronts us with the darkness of our shadow and the pain of our rejected self, this encounter with the collective will force us to acknowledge the anguish caused by our Western culture. And we will have to accept that we are the perpetrators of this suffering. We cannot blame anyone else, neither governments nor corporations. It is our collective shadow we are confronting.

Only when we confront the darkness with honesty and humility can we hope to transform it. Denial and arrogance subtly pull us into their web where we forget what is real. We need to accept our responsibility, to acknowledge that both individually and collectively we have created this dark monster which devours our light. We carry in our blood the sins of the culture we are born into—the people of the United States still carry the violence of the slaughter of the Native Americans. If we do not accept our collective responsibility, our light cannot penetrate the darkness; we cannot fully engage in the fight for our future. Inwardly we remain on the sidelines, spectators rather than full participants.

There are many ways to avoid and escape the darkness, many patterns of denial. But if we are sincere we will be taken to the places in the collective darkness in the inner and outer worlds where it is our duty to work, where our light can be used most effectively. Many mystics now live in the center of worldly life. Faded memories of spiritual seclusion may haunt us, but instead of living in the monastery we may find ourselves on Wall Street; instead of living in *ashrams*, we bring our remembrance to the inner cities. And in our meditation, or during the night when the soul is free from physical restrictions, we are guided to places of darkness where our light can help untangle webs of greed, penetrate clouds of ignorance. Sometimes we awake from a dream half-remembering or dreaming of the denseness, the heaviness that has been around us. One friend dreamed of walking city streets between vast sinkholes full of people caught in unconsciousness and forgetfulness. Another friend was present in a desolate, arid desert she knew to be caused by our culture.

On both the inner and outer planes we can help to create pathways of light where others can follow more easily. We can bring our integrity into the places of deceit and duplicity. We do not realize how these collective forces distort our general perception, how difficult it is to see clearly in this collective darkness. We breathe an air that is polluted and it subtly corrupts and contaminates our natural way of being. And we hardly recognize that this is happening.

It is important to understand that darkness is waiting to be transformed; its time of oppression is waning. While on the surface the darkness may appear to be strong, its structures of power belong to the past. At the end of any era there are forces that dissolve the passing age. This reflects the underlying laws of creation. In the organic wholeness of life even the darkness follows the cycles of creation and dissolution.

Just as our belief systems appear to be changing, so are the ways the darkness is held. The underpinnings of our whole collective way of life have been removed— which is why we sense a fundamental instability and insecurity. And this affects our collective shadow as well as our conscious relationship to life. In fact it is in the unconscious that changes first happen, as deep archetypal shifts take place.

Living at the end of an era is exhilarating and demanding. The archetypal patterns that give a sense of meaning and stability to life change. This is part of the pattern of evolution. Many people try to hold onto past ideologies and values, while others are drawn into the new currents of life. This creates tension and conflict, and can even evoke repression as those in power try to retain their positions. This too is a natural part of the cycle of change. But the new forces of life cannot be stopped; they are too primal and powerful. Working against them will simply provoke antagonism and unnecessary conflict, and yet this is also part of the process. Some people cannot help but hold onto the past; those most fixed in their ideas have the most to lose.

Working with the energy of the future is dangerous because there is no map. But there is a quality of joy and excitement that belongs to new life. Staying within the confines of the past may give the illusion of security, but it is countered by a growing sense of insecurity easily projected into the fear of terrorism or other forces outside of our control. On a physical level our present life is far safer compared with past centuries; we have conquered many diseases and have greater material comfort. But we do not feel any more secure in this safety, rather it appears to constellate greater fear. We sense there are shifts that we cannot understand or control, that the very fabric of life is changing.

This new life needs the darkness; otherwise it will not be whole. In the drama of life there have to be both light and darkness. But we need to work with the darkness in a new way: our collective denial and forgetfulness have created a powerful global monster of greed and abuse. The servants of life are working to change the way the darkness is constellated, so that it too will flow with the new energy of life. Fully confronting the darkness, they are sowing seeds of light in its depths, bringing sparks of remembrance into the centers of forgetfulness. There is a resistance to this work, but one cannot stop the flow of new life. This is not some minor event, but a primal shift in the spiritual and organic structure of the whole of creation.

CONNECTIONS OF LIGHT

At this time of transition the light of the soul of the world has a new vibration; it carries the consciousness of a new era. Certain places on the inner and outer planes where this light used to be directly accessed have been hidden; certain new places are to be revealed. And the work requires a new attitude. It can no longer be performed in seclusion, in places separate from the flow of outer events. The soul of the world can now be most directly accessed in the marketplace of life, where the dense energies of everyday life give a body to its higher frequencies. The light can now be spun into a fine thread that is indestructible and can be woven into the most ordinary clothes.

Because it functions on the frequency of oneness, this thread of light has the capacity to link together people of all different walks of life. And it needs these links to flow more freely. As these connections are made, the light of the soul of the world can flow where it needs to go. The prostitute on the street corner, the banker in his office, the poet with his phrases can all be directly connected, just as the internet can connect people of all types and all countries. There are no borders or boundaries to the work of this light, and the darkness is also included. To work with this light requires an openness of mind and a freedom from conditioning. We cannot afford to be constricted by past forms or barriers. There is a great joy in this coming together, in being connected through oneness and the light of the world.

In the light of oneness everything is included and life itself will celebrate this coming together, this linking without boundaries. Life is longing to be made whole, to have its essential nature recognized. Through the connections made by this light, life can flow in new ways, and expand our consciousness.

At first individual connections are made, from person to person, from soul to soul, and then these connections come alive and work with their own purpose. We think that a connection is a static line between two points, but a real connection brings a third function. It links the meanings of two individuals to create a new meaning, beyond that of the two individuals, a meaning that belongs to the moment of meeting. This third function has a life of its own beyond that of the two individuals and can relate directly to the whole. This is how something comes alive in a new way, through a meeting that takes us into a new dimension.

One of the limitations of our present understanding of the internet is that we have not fully realized the new dynamic created by the many new connections that are being made. We do not recognize that it is the connections themselves that are most important, not the information or goods that are exchanged. When these connections come alive, then the internet will wake to its real potential.

Part of our problem is that the nurturing and meaning of relationships traditionally belong to the feminine, and we have not included this understanding that is natural to women in our technological progress. We are still working primarily within a masculine analytic paradigm, rather than fully integrating the wisdom of the feminine. The feminine kind of knowing has a crucial role to play in the development of this technology.

The soul of the world has the blueprint for the connections that need to be made. These connections are not random, but follow a particular pattern and purpose. In our own lives we know the sudden potency of a meeting that seemed "meant to happen," whether with a teacher, a new love, or an old friend. There can be a shock of recognition, a feeling of wholeness, or the sense that something was given or received.

These connections need to be experienced consciously and with attention; otherwise their purpose will be lost. We must recognize them as important opportunities, even if we don't fully understand them. Some connections will work easily, while others may require persistence. Some individuals who are too identified with a particular mind-set will be resistant to certain connections. But through these connections the light of the soul of the world can flow into new places and awaken individuals to its work. As the pattern of connections grows, it will constellate new patterns for life, for the evolving consciousness of the planet. It is through the connections of individuals and groups that the consciousness of oneness will penetrate our collective consciousness and give form to the future.

This blueprint is not static or preordained, but reflects the organic nature of life. However, certain principles need to be followed, certain energies brought together. For example, over the last few years specific spiritual energies have been connected on the inner planes. This has been part of the creation of the web of light around the world. Some of these inner connections have been brought to the surface, making outer connections. Such connections are a real energetic exchange, a linking of the spiritual energies of specific spiritual traditions. This linking does not dilute the individual nature of each tradition, but creates a node of power that can facilitate further connections.

The transition from an inner to an outer connection is not always easy—in the outer world there are the problems caused by misunderstandings and ego dynamics that do not exist on the inner planes. As the transition takes place from the inner to the outer, more groups and paths can be connected. Many groups and individuals do not have conscious access to the inner planes and therefore can be connected together only in the outer world.

The inner planes and their workings have been hidden from most people in the West; even many spiritual paths do not know how to work directly in the inner planes. So either their consciousness needs to be attuned to this inner connection or the connection can be made solely in the outer.

If spiritual groups or individuals are receptive, it is possible to give them a quality of light that can connect them to the inner web of light. Otherwise a simple human connection can be made. Often this connection needs to be made from person to person. Although e-mail and the telephone offer wonderful means of communication, on the physical plane something can be exchanged from person to person, from heart to heart, that cannot be communicated over distance.

Through these connections the light of the soul of the world awakens a new consciousness in those who are accessible. And this light *is* the connection—these connections are an aspect of its nature. As the light comes alive in humanity, it awakens the connections that belong to oneness. What is fascinating is how this light has a life of its own, making the connections it needs. There are guardians of the light, and helpers who work with its unfolding. But the light itself knows where it needs to go, the connections it needs to make.

UNDERSTANDING THE FLOW OF LIGHT

Working with the light of the world is an underlying aspect of our shift towards a global awareness. This work is global, and yet it also includes the potential to interact with energies beyond our world. This is a hidden aspect of the next stage of our evolution. Global awareness means taking responsibility for our planet as a single living organism, which then means we will have the capacity to relate to other celestial organisms. Our world is a small part of a vast unfolding whole, each part interacting and affecting the whole. The predicament of our planet is our pressing concern, but as we step out of the image of separation into unity, we will emerge into a very different experience of our world. These changes we are experiencing are far more fundamental and far-reaching than we envision.

Part of this transition is an understanding of how different levels of reality interact. Even to acknowledge the existence of the light of the world is to accept an inner reality beyond our physical senses. Learning how to work with this inner energy, how to participate in its unfolding, will bring together the inner and outer world. We will experience how the light flows from the inner and nourishes the outer before being reflected back into the inner. The symbol of the number eight, with the two circles flowing into each other, is an image for this next stage of human awareness. Understanding the way that the energy flows is essential to our development. Many forms of healing are based upon an understanding of how energy flows in the body. There is less understanding of how the life force originates beyond the physical and comes into the physical plane, although forms of healing and energy work that work with the etheric body function at the intersection of the physical and non-physical plane.

But the first step is to be open and receptive to this inner light, and to work with the connections that it needs to make within the world. As these connections are made our consciousness will expand—these connections are the pathways of our global consciousness. The connections will open us to a larger understanding and the knowledge that we need in order to function at a global, multidimensional level. Humanity is the consciousness of the planet; we carry this divine gift in our individual and collective awareness. Linking together, we connect centers of awareness within our global brain, and this enables the energy to flow in new ways and a new level of awareness to develop. The internet is a part of the development of our global awareness, which is why its ability to make connections is so important. It is a web of connections being woven within the fabric of the world, although it does not exist at a solely physical level, but on an energy level we call cyberspace.

The way that the internet has developed reflects the way that oneness can work exponentially, without being constricted by past patterns of development. It follows the blueprint of the future, which is based upon oneness. In just a few years we have been given a new tool for relating globally and also directly from individual to individual. What is exciting is how it bypasses so many of the restrictions of the past, the power structures and "red tape" that try to control or limit any new development. It is alive in a new way. And this is just the beginning of this new stage of evolution.

We are now being asked to participate in life on different levels: on the interconnected plane of the soul, where we are all one, and on the outer stage where this oneness needs to be brought into our collective consciousness and our everyday life. Without the light of the soul of the world, this work cannot happen—the light carries the knowledge of oneness and the energy of oneness that we need. The light of the soul needs to heal and redeem what has been desecrated, penetrate places of darkness and worldly power. And it has to make many new connections as it helps the world awaken.

It is important to remember that this light is not other than our light. In the patriarchal era we focused on a transcendent God, which limited our direct access to this light. The light of the soul belonged in heaven with God. Now we have to embrace the light and bring it into life. We are the connections that need to be made, the pathways of the future. In our relating we carry the seeds of our collective development, which is why women have such a central role to play. Women understand more fully the importance of relating, how we are all connected together and form part of a whole. They carry these connections in their physical and spiritual bodies in a way that is foreign to men. On a higher level some women are able to magnetize these interconnections with a spiritual energy or substance, which enables the connections that are being made to directly communicate at the level of oneness. This means that when these human connections are made, the individual can awaken more quickly to the consciousness of oneness.

The light of the soul of the world needs the participation of all who are open to this work. But part of our redemption of the feminine is to acknowledge that certain work can only be done by women. The interconnections of life belong to the wisdom of the feminine and a woman's body holds the knowledge of how the worlds interrelate. Masculine consciousness imaged a transcendent divinity—the feminine knows how the divine is present in every cell of creation. Women know this not as abstract knowledge, but part of their instinctual nature—in the womb the light of a soul can come into physical form. Life is standing at the edge of an abyss of forgetfulness waiting for the light of the world to be born. This birth needs the wisdom of the feminine, and women must take their place in this time of great potential.

THE MAGIC OF LIFE

*There is one thing that we are certain about
and that is that we are all surrounded by a profound
mystery. And in some strange way we are asked to
participate in this mystery and to collaborate with it.*

Cecil Collins[1]

WHERE INNER AND OUTER MEET

Magic is life awake.

Magic is born between the worlds, where the inner and outer meet. It is part of the mysterious relationship of the Creator and creation, how the inner flows into life and back again. Working at this interface between the worlds, His servants can help creation to come alive with a new energy. At its highest level this energy is that of divine remembrance, a conscious aligning of life with its source. When creation remembers its Creator, it brings the joy of the soul into life. The joy of the soul will redeem and heal life at its deepest level. This belongs to the evolutionary shift that we are waiting for.

Magic is a part of life, existing in all moments, not just times of change. Without it, life slowly becomes separated from its source in the unseen and dies. Magic is needed to realign life, to help life to remember its higher purpose. By learning the ways of magic, we can help heal and redeem life, bring back life's joy.

In order to begin to understand how magic works, we have to recognize that the outer, physical world is part of many interdependent levels of reality, all of which affect each other. The harmonious interrelationship of these levels of reality is important to life's well-being. Just as an individual can become out of balance, so can the whole of life. If an individual becomes cut off from her soul, life loses its meaning; a quality of light becomes missing. Without this light the individual can easily become depressed, sick, or addicted to self-destructive patterns of behavior. This is also true of the whole. In our focus on ourselves we have forgotten that life as a whole can lose its connection with its deepest purpose and become depressed.

We are the guardians of the planet, and its spiritual and physical well-being is our responsibility. In order to fully embrace this responsibility, we need to know how the inner and outer affect each other, how the energy flows between the worlds. Life that is cut off from its deepest meaning will not flow creatively; it will not adapt and change in a creative way, but slowly spiral into patterns of self-destruction. Life has already constellated patterns that are unhealthy and negative. These negative patterns affect all living creatures, including humanity. In some instances negative energy dynamics have become so strong that life energies have inverted, turning back upon themselves, rather than flowing outward.

These negative energy patterns have already begun to affect life, as life-forms become depleted or die out. Entire ecosystems are unbalanced or near extinction, and the planet as a whole suffers from the destruction of the ozone layer, and depletion of its own self-sustaining energy sources.

We think that these phenomena are caused by pollution and ecological imbalance. We do not realize the depths of the problem, and how it cannot be addressed on a solely physical level. Magic is desperately needed to reverse these negative energy patterns, to alter the

THE GOLDEN SUFI CENTER
PO Box 428
Inverness, CA 94937-0428
USA

THE GOLDEN SUFI CENTER® publishes books and tapes on Sufism and mysticism. *Spiritual Power* is part of a new series of books on the emerging global consciousness of oneness. Other books in this series include *Light of Oneness* and *Working with Oneness*. For further information, please visit www.workingwithoneness.org. Please return this card, or visit www.goldensufi.org for further information about The Golden Sufi Center.

TO ORDER any of the following please check the appropriate box. For US orders: media-mail shipping (2-3 weeks) is $4 for first item and $1 for each additional item, first-class shipping (3-10 days) is $8 for first item and $2 for each additional. CA residents add 7.25% sales tax. To order by mail return this card with check or money order. Order by phone or fax (VISA & MasterCard only) tel 415-663-8773, fax -9128, 9AM - 5PM PT, Monday - Friday.

by LLEWELLYN VAUGHAN-LEE
□ *Light of Oneness* - $14.95
□ *Working with Oneness* - $14.95

by IRINA TWEEDIE
□ *Daughter of Fire* - $19.95

by HILARY HART
□ *The Unknown She* - $15.95

NAME ....

ADDRESS ....

CITY / STATE / ZIP ....

PHONE ....

EMAIL ....

□ Check here to be placed on the mailing list.

SP-2005

way the energy constellates. But our patriarchal culture killed its magicians long ago; only a few shamans are left. And the realms of magic themselves are littered with the refuse of our own desires and self-interest, making it more difficult to access their nourishment.

How can we bring the healing energy of the unseen into life? Is there a way to bypass all of the difficulties that we have created and restore life to balance and well-being? The primal unity of life is always present and has its own magic. Because we are a part of this oneness, we can each have direct access to life's magic. We do not have to be dependent upon the intercession of priests or undergo the intense training of the shaman. There is a new way to access magic in the midst of life and through the ways of oneness to work with this magic. But in order to do this work we have to step out of our present paradigm of separation and isolation.

The energy of life follows thought. If we see ourself as separate from the whole, existing in a solely physical world, we cannot use the magic of life. It will not flow through us. But once we recognize that we are an integral part of a multidimensional creation, we can use the magic that is inherent in all of life to heal and transform. We are the cocreators of our own destiny, working with the divine energy that is present within all levels of existence and nonexistence.

THE MAGICAL SUBSTANCE OF CREATION

Part of the heritage of humanity is to be able to access the places where the inner and outer meet and to work here with magic. We need to redeem magic and learn how it works with the wholeness of life. This is part of our responsibility as the guardians of life.

Opening ourselves to magic means that we will become open to a new dimension of ourselves and of life. We will not have to exist in a solely physical world, but can reclaim the magical landscape of our ancient ancestors. This will create new opportunities and unexpected dangers, just as our exploration of the physical world brought both treasures and disease. But without access to this magic, humanity will starve from lack of meaning and the world will become a desecrated wilderness. We need to bring the simple magic of life back into the marketplace, and open ourselves to new ways of being.

We feel how magic is a part of life in the miracle of birth when something simple and miraculous takes place. We sense magic in a rainbow, whose unexpected colors shine out of a gray sky. We feel it in a chance meeting with a friend we haven't seen for years. Or when a problem that seemed unsolvable suddenly resolves itself or becomes insignificant. If we recognize these moments, they can bring unexpected joy, and awaken something deep within us. These feelings are not fantasy, but signs of a real meeting between the inner and the outer, signs that we have entry to the unexpected beyond the dullness of our habits and obligations.

The unseen world is all around us, helping us, speaking to us through synchronicities and dreams. We belong in the inner worlds, in the wonder of what is hinted at but not yet visible. Our own life is part of a flow of energy from the inner to the outer; every breath follows this rhythm. We are the meeting of the worlds, which is why human beings have the potential to make everything sacred, to bring alive the mystery of divine remembrance in each and every breath.

To be alive to magic is to be alive to the hidden potential of life. Life does not need to follow the laws of reason or linear thinking. Even the laws of nature cannot limit life. Life has a substance that can allow the unexpected to happen. When we participate directly with this hidden substance, we can weave patterns of magic into the fabric of creation. We can bring colors and fragrances from the inner worlds into the outer, and work to free life of its present constrictions. We can sense the gifts that are offered in every moment, gifts which draw us deeper and deeper into the endless possibilities of what is real.

> Every moment wears a robe with ten thousand
>   pockets.
> And every pocket holds more than a million
>   possibilities.[2]

The magical substance of creation is no longer an esoteric secret. It used to be hidden in arcane texts and mysterious symbols, accessed only through rituals. But as certain veils between the worlds are removed, we will find that this substance is something simple and ordinary. It belongs to the moment when energy becomes matter, when the unseen takes on the visible manifestation of form. It brings to life the colors of creation, the wonder that is the manifest world. It gives meaning to everyday activities and reveals the ordinary as sacred.

Humanity can be present between the outer and the inner and participate in the workings of life's magic. We do not need to be bound by the rules of the rational, but can be alive in the spontaneous happenings of the moment. Through our hearts and minds we can guide the way life happens. We can give our personal magic to life and be awake to the magic of the whole of creation.

What will become most apparent is the simplicity of magic. We may think that magic is evoked by complicated incantations, but the magic of life is as simple as breathing, and is discovered through being attentive at the meeting of the inner and outer. The inner is longing to be recognized; its real potential wants to be used. The outer is waiting to come awake. We are the place where the worlds can come together and our consciousness is the catalyst. Through our consciousness the outer can awaken to the purpose and meaning of the inner and so life can reveal itself. This is true magic. Through this conscious meeting many things can happen.

THE SPARK OF CONSCIOUSNESS

Magic comes alive when the spark of human consciousness is given to the whole. In service to life we help awaken life to its magical nature. Through the spark of our consciousness, creation is revealed as a dazzling spectacle of light upon light.

There is a way to work with magic that until now has been inaccessible. This belongs to the way consciousness can interact with the energy of creation before it constellates into form. Energy from the inner flows into form through the energy patterns of life. These patterns are becoming accessible in a new way that enables consciousness to directly interact with them and subtly shift the way energy is constellated. Working with the flow of energy, we can use our attention to put a spark into the moment of transformation from energy into form. This allows the dynamic of creation to respond in a new way.

The spark of consciousness is His gift to humanity, and it is this gift that makes us guardians of the planet.

Our work is to give this spark of consciousness back to creation so that it can help the world to come alive. In our present stage of evolution we have used this gift mainly for our own self-interest, for our survival and the gratification of our desires. This use of consciousness has taken us to the point of destroying our ecosystem and each other. We need to give it back to the whole of life.

This belongs to the next stage of our evolution. Global consciousness means that we give our consciousness back to life for the sake of the whole. This is not an idea but a real interaction in which our spark of consciousness participates directly with the outer world. It is beautiful to see—light flows from an individual into life, awakening life to its own light. We don't need to know exactly what we are doing. But our attention must be shifted away from ourselves so that our love and consciousness can flow outward, free from the back-eddies where our self-obsession has entrapped it. We have to recognize that we are no longer the center of our world. This is as basic and revolutionary as Galileo's awareness that the earth goes around the sun rather than the sun's circling the earth.

When our spark of consciousness is given in service to the whole, life will respond in ways that are not presently available. Our consciousness is the catalyst that can awaken new energy centers and new ways for energy to flow into life. We know how this happens in our own inner journey when we turn our attention away from the desires of the ego. Our consciousness then opens us to the miraculous that is always present but hidden by our ego. And consciousness itself begins to change and expand. It no longer follows the patterns of our conditioning but awakens to its higher purpose.

We do not recognize the real potential of consciousness. Consciousness is our divine gift and it can function in many different ways on many different levels. It carries the seeds of the future, but these seeds need to be given to life; otherwise they cannot grow. The simple act of giving our consciousness in service to the whole is the spark that will transform the world. And because we are an integral part of the whole, life itself will show us where we are needed—not the life that exists on a solely physical level, but life that flows from the inner to the outer and carries the imprint of its divine nature.

When life is awake it will respond quite differently from its present sleeping state. But there is no savior outside of ourself who can bring about this change—"We are the ones we have been waiting for." It is our participation that is needed, a participation that on its highest level recognizes the divinity that is within everything. When we remember Him and witness His presence, when we see His oneness in the many, we align life to what is real and bring this reality into life.

And yet there is always the sadness of leaving behind our childhood state in which we played the part of children in relation to a parental image of God or some other authority figure. To step into the role of responsibility is a sacrifice some are unwilling to make. But only through the acceptance of our responsibility can our own consciousness awake to its potential and go where it is needed. Children are always waiting for someone to tell them what to do, even if they rebel against it. In the reality of oneness we are working together—there is no external authority. Oneness works quite differently from the authoritarian power structures of the past era. There is the need of the moment and our ability to respond to this need. It is very simple and direct.

IN SERVICE TO THE ONENESS OF LIFE

In the space where the worlds come together we can participate directly in the process of creation. Our consciousness is like a masculine spark and the substance of life the feminine that receives it. Through their union something new can be born, a way of life that acknowledges the unity of creation not as an abstract idea but a lived reality. When life knows its oneness, its energy can flow more freely and new forms of life come into being. These will be organic relationships between the individual life-forms that are already here. These integrated dynamic relationships will be a new form of life in themselves. In our present conditioning we imagine a new form of life as something separate, but the internet points to an evolving form of interrelationships that itself is becoming an organic life-form, although at present it has not yet become fully alive.

Through the patterns of interrelationship life can reclaim its oneness on a new level. And because this oneness is a reflection of divine oneness, it can carry a new quality of divine consciousness—His gift of consciousness can evolve to a new level. But these patterns of relationship cannot function on a solely outer level. They need to include the inner; otherwise the magic that is vital to life will be missing. Inner and outer have to work together, and the spark of consciousness is vital to this process. We are needed at the place where the worlds meet to seed this new level of evolution.

Those who have been drawn inward know the wonders of the inner world. We have seen its landscapes of light in our dreams and visions, heard its celestial music, carried its fragrance into our lives. We have learned to be nourished by the inner while we live in a world that seems to have forgotten its existence. But as yet we have understood this inner connection mainly in terms of our personal development, how our dreams can guide us on our journey, how the healing energies or beauty of the inner can bring nourishment to our life. We have not understood how our participation with the inner is needed to nourish the whole, how it can activate certain energy structures within the whole of life that will reconnect us all.

When I was first working with the inner world I was told by an inner figure:

> Each time you come from your world to this inner world, and you come with love and understanding, not greed, then a grain of sand has crossed the great divide. However small it may be, that grain of sand has immense meaning because it comes with love. It forms part of a vast pattern, like a mandala, and when this pattern is complete then there will be a healing beyond all healing as the outer returns to the inner and Self reveals itself. Then a new life will be upon your earth and upon my earth and there will be a flowering as there has not been for thousands of years.

If we can recognize that our individual connection with the inner is part of this larger pattern, this mandala of wholeness that is being formed, we can step into the true dimension of this work. Our longing, dreams, or creativity do not draw us into the inner just for ourselves, but for the sake of the whole. In the inner where nothing has been crystallized into a fixed identity, everything is connected in the fluid interplay of energy and forms. Here the pulsating oneness of creation is more apparent.

Through our participation, life will regenerate itself, form new patterns of relationships through which the energy of life will flow freely, purify, heal, and transform and activate certain energy centers. Within our consciousness there is a knowing of oneness that is needed by life. This is the spark of the consciousness of the new era which creation needs to evolve. Without our participation the degradation of life will continue.

When we are caught in patterns of complexity, it is difficult to recognize the simplicity of this transformation. We see what appear as complex problems surrounding us, and many of these problems are real and cause suffering. We hardly dare to realize that we are the solution, that our consciousness contains the catalyst for real transformation. But once we enter into the consciousness of oneness, we see a different picture in which each part is dependent upon the pattern of relationships that bind us all together. These patterns are born in the inner worlds and come into physical form through the energy of creation. Only human beings can step freely from the outer to the inner. Spirits and angels belong to the inner worlds, while animals exist in the outer world. Only humans can work between the worlds where magic is born.

We are a part of life and respond to its calling. We are drawn to the inner because life needs us to make this connection. Once we acknowledge this dimension of our inner work, we can begin to see how we have all come together at this time of need and thus glimpse the mandala that is being formed. Certain barriers that at present are limiting this work will then fall away. It is not easy to break out of our identification with our individual self, with its journey and self-development. This is the powerful imprint of our conditioning. But we are all part of a whole that is in its birth pains, as a new way of being struggles to come alive.

FIGURES OF THE INNER WORLDS

Working between the worlds, we will find something unexpected and wonderful. We will meet the friends who are here to help, the inner figures of love and guidance who have been waiting for us. Sometimes we have seen them in our dreams, the wise old man or knowing child who points out the way. These figures are real, but we have turned away from them in our focus on the outer. They know the ways of magic, how the mysterious can take place. They can not only guide us, but teach us how the forces of life unfold, how we can work with life's invisible energy lines and learn to be in the right place at the right time. They know how the energy flows from the inner to the outer, how to keep open the pathways of light. They understand the patterns of relationship that bind the worlds together, and how to live in harmony with these patterns. Without these friends it would take us a thousand years to understand how the inner works, how to bring its magic into our life. But through recognizing and relating to them, our consciousness will make a real connection to a forgotten part of our inner nature.

Without the help of these inner figures we would be lost in the maze of the inner. We would stumble down passageways not knowing which door to open. They know where our treasures are hidden and have the keys we need to gain entrance. Because they are unable to cross freely into the outer world, they have to wait for us to come to them. But once we are present between the worlds they can take us by the hand and teach us their wisdom. They understand the symbolic structure of life, and how images of power can be used. They can show us swords that cut through illusions and sacred flowers that can cure the sickness of the soul. They can help us to remember our forgotten selves, and how to use the magic that is our inner heritage.

There are many ways to communicate and work with these inner figures. They are easily accessed through the imagination, our faculty for communicating with the inner, symbolic world.[3] Through the imagination we can see in the inner world and meet with its inhabitants. Some people need to dance their meeting, while others may tell stories, sing, or paint them. These figures are similar to the magical animals in the cave paintings in southern France, who are the guardians of the chase. They are also imaged in the animal and bird-headed masks of tribal dances. In their different forms they have been painted, danced, and sung for thousands of years. Only recently have we discarded them, dimly remembering them in dreams and children's stories. But without their presence we remain stranded in the outer world, dependent only upon our effort and without access to the realms of magic.

These inner figures can interpret for us the play of outer events, so that we understand their real significance and how to work with these events. They can point to the places of trouble and the sources of nourishment and healing. They can shield us from forces that might disturb or torment us; they may even battle for us in the darkness. Without their guardianship we would be left alone, vulnerable to many unseen forces, not knowing where to go in the pathways between the worlds. When we communicate with them, another dimension becomes part of our life.

We each have our own inner guardians and guides, power animals and protective figures. They are a part of our unique individual inner nature as well as being inhabitants of the inner worlds. They are not always good. Some people have mischievous figures who play tricks on their outer life. They can disrupt events or up-set a well-planned schedule, especially if their presence is ignored. In the past such an inner figure was known as a daemon, an attendant spirit. Through our behavior these figures can also become corrupted, become demons who draw us further into darkness. Our outer and inner life directly affect them. We can nourish or starve them, bring them light or darkness. They are an integral part of our psyche, and often carry part of our life force.

Through relating to these imaginal figures we make a conscious connection with the inner world. This in-teraction is part of the bridge that is being built, the mandala that is being formed. When this work is com-plete, it forms a union of opposites, what the alchemists called *coniunctio oppositorum*. This will give birth within us to the child who belongs to the future. This is the child with stars in her eyes who knows the deep rhythms of life that belong to both the seen and the unseen worlds. She is the archetype of oneness that is being given as a gift to each of us. For each of us she is unique, and she is also part of the being of the whole world.

THE MOVEMENT OF MAGIC

Magic has a movement, a way of coming into being that is alive. Magic is not something we do, but something that is, and in its being there are currents of energy that affect life. Working with magic is a way of participating in life in harmony with this energy, an energy in which certain dynamics of the inner worlds are brought directly into the outer. The magus is one who knows how to be in this flow of energy, who is attuned to it. The magus is not constricted by the patterns of outer life, but can move with the energy of the inner as it is present in the outer.

How can we learn about the movement of magic and become attuned to its flow? One of the easiest ways is to leave behind our dualistic thinking which suggests that magic is something other. We are all magical beings, just as we all have dreaming selves who can change shapes, fly, or breathe underwater. Magic and its movement are a part of us. Just as we need to reclaim our understanding of the symbolic language of dreams, we need to reclaim our magical nature. We need to be present between the worlds where our magic is most accessible. In these spaces we will discover our own quality of magic, our own way of moving with its energy.

Magic is not a trick, but an energy that belongs to life and can make things happen. In our culture personal magic is often mistaken for charisma or personal magnetism. Charisma attracts people's attention and one can use this energy to bring people together and to influence them. But there is another dimension to personal magic which requires an understanding of its origin between the worlds and how it can work with the symbolic nature of life. Symbols are not just images but transformers of energy which give us access to the primal energies of life without them overwhelming us with their raw power. They function in a similar way to an electrical transformer that lowers the energy from a power plant so that it can be used in ordinary domestic equipment without blowing it up. The Catholic mass is a clear example of this function of symbols. Through the symbolic ritual of bread and wine the recipient is able to eat of the body and drink of the blood of Christ, in other words to be nourished by the divine energy of the Christ, and take this energy of the sacrament back into ordinary everyday life.

Part of the present shift in evolution is that we are being given the ability and knowledge to discover our own symbols and learn how to work with them. There are many different ways to discover our own symbols, through visualizations, guided meditations, dreamwork, painting, music, dance, and other forms of self-exploration. How to use these symbols, how to access their magic qualities in our daily life, is less understood.

A symbol can give us direct access to the inner world, and enable us to be nourished by its energy. We are then able to live closer to the source of life and with access to an energy that has not yet been constricted by physical form or desecrated. But we have to respect the symbolic world and allow it to reveal to us its ways. We cannot impose our needs and desires upon the symbolic—use it just to get what we want. Otherwise we will only continue our pattern of rape, desecration, and pollution. Unfortunately there are many recently popularized techniques of using the imagination in this way, to constellate and manifest our desires. We can see the ecological destruction caused by this ego-centered attitude towards the physical world. Its effect upon the inner imaginal world will also have far-reaching negative consequences.

RESPECT

In the coming years many ways of working with the symbolic world will become known to us. This is part of the knowledge of the coming era that is gradually being made accessible. We will have the opportunity to make our own relationship with our symbolic nature, discover its ways and allow it to teach us how to work with its energies. We will learn how to reestablish a symbolic consciousness through which all of life is an interaction with the divine, a meeting of the inner and outer worlds.[4] What is important is the attitude we bring to this work, that we are in service to the whole rather than following our ego and imposing its desires.

Working with the inner world requires listening, patience, and receptivity. One must allow the inner to communicate in its own way: watch, listen, and be responsive to the feelings that are evoked. This is the ancient wisdom of the feminine, which has been so repressed. Part of this deep wisdom is also respect. In previous eras it was understood that through our symbolic consciousness we are given access to the world of the gods.[5] The gods should be approached with respect.

We also need to bring an attitude of humility, because we are encountering a world as ancient as the universe which contains the wisdom of the ages. Inteacting with the inner world, we are the ones who need guidance and help. The ego should not try to determine the outcome of such a meeting. Indeed there is a particular danger for those who approach the inner world without the "wisdom of humility." Carl Jung called this "inflation," when the ego identifies with the energy of the inner. It is easy for the ego to think that it is all-powerful, that it is a magician. The story of Doctor Faustus tells of the danger of using magic for the power purposes of the ego.

The inner world is a source of unlimited energy and power. The ego can become attracted by this and try to use it for its own purposes. Entering the inner world, we are exploring a new dimension, and there is the potential for the wondrous and unexpected. But for this encounter to be fruitful, the right attitude is necessary. If one meets a unicorn one should not try to cut off its horn for its magical properties, but rather greet the wondrous animal with respect. Many fairy tales stress that the attitude with which we approach the figures of the inner world determines their response. The stepdaughter who greets the gnomes with kindness is rewarded with magical gifts, while the daughter who seeks these figures for greed receives a curse.

In previous ages it was only the initiates who were allowed direct access to the inner worlds. Part of their training was a process of purification and testing to determine whether they had the correct attitude. The elders knew the dangers—not just to the individual but to the whole community—of interacting with the inner worlds with the wrong attitude. If we are to reclaim our relationship to the inner, to learn to live our magical nature, we need to take full responsibility for our attitude and our actions in the outer and inner worlds.

What is not generally known is that many places in the inner world are as polluted as the outer world. Our lack of respect for the inner has corrupted its magical realms. Every time we access the inner with a desire to get something for ourself, we desecrate it. Like the base camps of Mt. Everest, now littered with the refuse of hundreds of expeditions, our quest for a spiritual "high" has polluted the inner realms. Decades of this desecration, culminating in recent new-age practices that seem to encourage visiting the inner for the sake of one's own personal knowledge or gains, has left the inner worlds crowded with the garbage of spiritual materialism.

The dense wasteland of debris created by our own egos inhibits light and energy from flowing to the outer where it can bring nourishment and meaning into life. Forces that should flow outward turn back on themselves, contributing to the darkness and negativity of both worlds. The shamans, who were trained to keep the inner dimensions clean, have mostly disappeared. Now the only way to help clear out some of this pollution and open pathways between the inner and the outer is to approach the inner worlds with deep respect and humility, in service to the whole, wanting nothing for ourself.

THE MAGIC OF THE FUTURE

As humanity evolves, the ways of magic change. Magic is no longer in the hands of the initiates, accessed through esoteric diagrams and secret rituals. Magic now belongs to everyday life; this is where the energy and places of power are to be found. There is no purpose in trying to rediscover the old ways, translate the ancient texts. Through our direct participation with the inner world the new ways of magic will reveal themselves.

We need to redeem the wisdom of the feminine but we cannot return to the time of the priestess. The masculine and feminine have to work together; our actions in the outer world must be guided by our receptivity to the inner. And there is no hierarchy to this work. Part of the blueprint of the future is the ability of each individual to participate directly with the work of the whole. Magic belongs to all of life and to each of us. We can choose whether to use this magic, and also choose whether to follow the desires of our ego or the need of the whole. These choices are simple and will have direct consequences upon our own life and the life of the whole.

Without our participation the magic will not come alive. But we do not know how this magic will manifest, because until now it has been hidden, veiled from everyday awareness. As the veils between the worlds are lifted, magic will make her presence felt. She will speak to each of us in our own way—this is part of the wonder of oneness. And although magic follows exact laws, it also has a freedom from certain constrictions. Because it is born between the worlds, it is not limited by the patterns of either the inner or the outer. It is alive in a way that combines and transcends both.

And we must not forget the fun that belongs to magic. It carries the quality of the trickster, and can be full of jokes. Being open to magic means leaving behind a well-ordered sensible life, because magic likes to disrupt our plans, laugh at our pettiness, turn our life upside down. Magic does not like superficial morality or prejudice. It can be a mirror to reflect back to us what we do not like about ourselves. One cannot control magic with the laws of reason because it is continually slipping between the levels of reality, and can mock our good intentions with well-meaning laughter. There are good reasons that the self-righteous Puritans banned the magic of Merry England, which was imaged as Puck in *A Midsummer Night's Dream*, that "merry wanderer of the night," who makes us fall in love and play the part of an ass.

When we welcome back magic we will also find a sorrow that was caused by her banishment. Her absence has meant that a quality of life has been missing. We have become too sensible and restricted. Even our spiritual aspirations have become too well-meaning. When the Creator enters His own creation, He's not coming to save the world. He's not coming to make things right. He's coming because He wants to enjoy what He has created for Himself. And part of this enjoyment is His magical nature and the laughter of life that is filled with His presence.

How we respond to the presence of magic depends upon our own freedom and foolhardiness. Can we allow life to play tricks and slip out of our control? Can we respond to the moment without the fear of appearing foolish? Or would we rather remain in the safety of what we think we know, with our self-image well-protected? Magic is for those who say an unconditioned "Yes" to life, who dare to welcome the divine with its colors of the jester. It awakes us to what

> mostpeople fear most:
> a mystery for which i've
> no word except alive
>
> —that is,completely alert
> and miraculously whole;
>
> with not merely a mind and a heart
>
> but unquestionably a soul—[6]

THE ENERGY OF AWAKENING

He knows what enters the earth and what comes out of it,
and what descends from heaven and what rises up into it.
He is with you wherever you are.

Qur'an 57:4

Over the last decades the world has been gradually prepared for an evolutionary shift. The veils between the
inner and outer are becoming increasingly transparent,
allowing us access to new energies and understanding,
offering new opportunities to work with real power, like
working with the light of the soul of the world and with
the inner dimensions where magic comes alive.

But this is only a beginning. One of the limitations
of our present spiritual awareness is that many are identi-
fying these opportunities as the real thing, unaware that
they are only a preparation.

The changes taking place around and within us now
are caused by the gradual infusion of energy from the
unseen worlds. So much is becoming possible. We are
being given an awareness of the oneness of life, of how
we are all interconnected and need to help each other.
We are being given energy to help the world heal from
the wounds of the patriarchy, the pollution and other
ecological effects, and to heal the desecrated spirit of
humanity, which has forgotten the joy and the sanctity
of all of creation. The magic at the core of life is dancing
and sparkling at the edge of our vision.

These are profound and awe-inspiring changes.
However, the evolutionary shift that is coming cannot

be caused just by a gradual infusion of energy; it needs a direct influx of energy. Some energies from the inner world which are needed for our evolution can be filtered into our awareness, but others need to be given directly, so that their potency, vibration, and quality of light are not lost. Energy given directly can awaken the soul of the world, awaken us all to a new way of being.

Real change always comes from an influx of energy. For example, in the life of an individual the changes of adolescence come from the awakening of sexual energy. Changes that happen on the spiritual path are caused by the awakening of a different vibration of energy in our spiritual centers. Mostly such changes take place gradually as new energy is assimilated. However, there are also moments of instant awakening as a new energy is given directly to the individual.

On the spiritual path we know how such awakenings are wonderful but also unbalancing. The sudden awakening of the *kundalini* energy can bring states of bliss, ecstasy, and cosmic consciousness and also cause real psychological or mental imbalance. At such times we must be prepared to quickly let go of our past patterns of perception as we awaken to a vaster dimension. The help and guidance of a teacher who understands how such energy works are critical.

How this coming influx of energy will affect life is not predetermined. In many ways it is an experiment in evolution. Despite all the work of preparation it will be the receptivity of humanity at the moment the energy is given that will have a determining effect.

Those who have access to the inner worlds can be attuned to the energy before it comes into the outer. Part of the work of spiritual groups is to be inwardly prepared and to hold a receptive awareness in the midst of humanity, to learn not to be shocked or unbalanced by something very different from the known. They can also be inwardly trained to work with this energy, to bring it quickly into the collective with a minimum of disturbance. Their individual consciousness can be programmed with this new frequency so that when the energy comes into the outer they instinctively know what to do. They are aligned with this energy and know how it functions.

How we respond as a global community at the moment the energy flows into the world is crucial. To what degree will we resist the change or step into the new awareness? How easily can we let go of our past attitudes and be guided by what is given? Humanity has the free will to say "Yes" or "No." Those most entrenched in their patterns of power or ideologies will probably resist. Those who have already given themselves to God have nothing to lose. For the mass of humanity the choice is more precarious. There are signs that collectively we can quickly adapt to what is given, as in our accelerating global use of the internet. But we also have collective tendencies to resist any changes that might appear to threaten our status quo. The drive to protect our personal and national interests at the expense of the whole is a powerful force that resists any real shift towards global unity.

The new energy will come into our lives regardless of how we respond. We can be inwardly prepared but we cannot protect ourselves against it. The danger of resisting such a powerful influx of energy is not just that we deny its potential for change, but that in our attitude and actions we constellate patterns that are antagonistic to this new life force; thus we may become caught in unnecessary conflicts. The energy that will be given has a force that is necessary to bring about fundamental change. Because it belongs to oneness, it is an energy of harmony and balance, but in its immediacy there is a strength that could seem like violence. It also has a clarity and simplicity that belong to what *is*, which is very different from the shadowy power dynamics with which we are familiar.

How can one compare a world of half-truths and distortions with the light of dawn? In the light of this energy we will come to know ourselves as we really are, without pretense. We will be given an understanding of ecological patterns and of how energy flows on the inner planes. In the light of this new awareness, interpersonal relationships will also change—we will no longer be imprisoned in such a murky landscape of misunderstood projections. We will have to take more responsibility for ourselves on many levels.

Those who are free to be alive in this way will rejoice, while others who live only through their disguises and roles will feel unprotected, and as in the myth of Eden, afraid to be naked. The simplicity and directness of sunlight are not easy for everyone. But in this sunlight our pretenses will fall away as the essential nature of each individual will find its true function.

The energy that is about to be given belongs to life itself and has the potential to awaken life. Nothing is excluded and the unique nature of every aspect of creation is celebrated. This is how oneness works when it is not just a concept but a living presence. Many patterns and attachments that we think are essential to life will fall away, just as our present structures of power will become redundant. And the wonder of this change is that it need not be gradual, because it belongs to the *now*. Any real change is always a miracle—it happens through the grace of God.

THE PLACES OF POWER

Energy that will help shift our evolution will enter our world at the places of power. Places of power are where energies of the inner dimensions can come directly into outer life without being filtered or diffused. In past eras these places of spiritual power were often in isolated areas. For example, for centuries the mountains of Tibet were a locus of spiritual power. Sometimes, though, they were in the midst of outer life; for example, during the Renaissance Florence was a place of power, combining new inspiration with classical ideas to nourish our Western culture.

Because we are at the beginning of a new era, the ways that energy from the inner planes flows into the outer world are changing. Places of power are no longer necessarily fixed geographical locations. For example, they can be spiritual groups, whose attitude of surrender and service allows the inner to flow directly into the world, whose attunement to the needs of the whole can help guide energy where it is needed. In general, places of power are no longer isolated in deserts or mountains but are in the midst of humanity. It is here that the influx of energy will be given—directly into the social and economic structure of life.

Spiritual groups exist at these places of power and are being trained to work with the energies from the inner world, trained to hold this energy and bring it into the outer. Spiritual groups dedicated to service are the most effective. The more the attention of individuals or groups is focused on themselves, the less access they have to the energy that is being given to humanity as a whole. The way this energy will be used is quite different from the current use of energy and other resources accessible in the outer world, where corporations and governments direct it to their own or other special interests' benefit.

The energies of the new era need the participation of human consciousness to be reflected into life. At the places of power, the energy can be very concentrated. But human consciousness can learn to work with it. Part of the nature of the energy that is being given is that it carries a quality of consciousness—this is why it needs our individual consciousness. Like the mystery of "light upon light," the consciousness of this energy needs human consciousness in order to come fully into life. A group of spiritually awakened individuals, ideally those who are aligned with their higher self, can bring the full capacity of this energy directly into the world. The less aligned the individual, the less access she has to the full range of the inner energy.

Mystics who are trained to be in two worlds at once are needed in these places of power. Energy in the inner world moves much faster than energy in the outer world, where it is restricted by the density of the physical plane. When energy flows from the inner to the outer, it undergoes a shift in vibration; otherwise it would be spinning too fast to be accessible in the outer. In order to work with the energy of the inner dimensions, one must be present in both worlds. This is one of the reasons that mystics are most suited to this work—through their spiritual practices they connect to the inner, as their involvement in ordinary life grounds them in the outer. And their essential emptiness allows the energy of the inner to flow with a minimum of distortion, so it can be most effective in the world.

Because a group has access to the collective consciousness in a way that an individual does not, it is through the vehicle of spiritually awakened individuals within groups that the energy can be reflected most directly into the collective consciousness. A group of individuals can flow in and out of the collective more easily than a single individual who is limited by a distinct personal boundary. And the energy field of the group is a protection when it enters the collective, making it safer and more effective.

As energy from the unseen flows through our consciousness, it will gradually awaken us to the nature of the work. Until now most of this work has been hidden, even from the consciousness of those involved. Real spiritual work involves a quality of surrender in which we do not know how we are used:

> I do not ask to see.
> I do not ask to know.
> I ask only to be used.[1]

But now, although our inner attitude of service and surrender remains, we will become more conscious of how we are used, and be able to more consciously participate in this process. This awakening will be a big shift for many who are accustomed to being used unknowingly. The danger is that the ego might get hold of this knowledge and become inflated, or even invent images of spiritual work, but there is a shadow side to every venture. We need to recognize this danger and be attentive to the ego's seduction and power games. There is usually a warning when this is about to happen, in the form of either a dream or an outer event. But the danger should not stop our participation. To give oneself in service means to be fully attentive to the work.

ONENESS AND THE FLOW OF LIFE

Life is waiting for energy from the inner worlds—nothing else will heal and transform it. But the energy needs to be given in a way that nourishes life rather than overwhelms it. This is why spiritual groups are present at these places of power, working to contain and balance this energy and reflect it into life in a way that is beneficial. Mystics trained in this work are awake to how energy flows from the inner to the outer, and also how energy flows through the matrix of life. Those immersed in oneness are attuned to where the energy is needed by the whole, and can help guide it.

The energy of awakening is being given for the whole of life. If it is used for the sole benefit of individuals or groups, its full potential will not be accessible. Furthermore, if the energy is used for personal gain, it might have a destructive effect by fragmenting and corrupting those who use it. We know how an individual can become unbalanced or corrupted by worldly power. Spiritual power can be equally destructive and also more difficult to guard against as it is less visible and its effects less understood. It can cause inflation and psychological imbalance, but more subtle and dangerous are the ways it can corrupt the substance of the soul. Just as the ego can be corrupted by worldly power, so can our higher vehicles be corrupted by spiritual power. This distorts the inner perception and access to what is real.

On the outer stage an ego that has been corrupted is more susceptible to negative energies and forces of darkness. Corruption diminishes the ability to perceive clearly—one's vision is clouded. There is less light to see through the shadows of our projections and life's distortions. The same is true of the corruption of the soul, except that the negative energies that are then attracted belong to the inner worlds; they are more difficult to identify and move faster than in the outer world. Also, when the higher vehicles are corrupted, they lose the natural protection that belongs to the soul—its light is covered over.

Individual consciousness can be attuned to the whole and work in service to the needs of the whole. This is one of the qualities of consciousness that is being developed at this time. An awareness of the oneness of life is not an abstract idea but a lived reality in which all parts of the whole relate together. It is the relationship of the individual to the whole that is most important. Through this relationship the attention of the individual is drawn where it is needed, where her contribution can be most effective. This reflects the organic nature of life, in which each part relates directly to the whole. Life is self-organizing and self-nurturing, and the more we are open to this pattern of relating, the more our consciousness can be used.

But we must understand that it can take time to adjust our awareness. Often we don't see the patterns of how we are being used until long after the work is done. We can be involved in a project for months, and only later see how we were led, how our attention was put, seemingly by chance, in a specific direction. Sometimes we think we are just following a random hunch, when later we see the beautiful patterns and connections that were being made all along. We must learn not to expect dramatic "spiritual" guidance, but simply to allow an invisible hand to help weave the mystery into our efforts.

The oneness of being is fundamental to mystical consciousness. We know the divine oneness in which every particle of creation reflects the face of the Beloved:

In everything there is a witness
that points to the fact that He is One.

The paradox of mystical consciousness is that we live
our separation from this unity as well as our awareness of
belonging to it. The pain of separation that the mystic
experiences as longing grows from an awareness of the
primal unity that is imprinted within us. We know both
the wonder of the multiplicity of life and its inherent
oneness. We can simultaneously see both the parts and
the whole, and know how each part is a unique expression
of the oneness. This enables us to consciously participate
in the unfolding life of the whole.

The relationship between the one and the many
is one of the primal mysteries of creation. The vertical
axis of this relationship, how every particle of creation
praises God, is experienced by many mystics. What is
less understood is the horizontal axis of the dynamics of
oneness, how all the parts of the whole relate together
in an expression of their divine nature. This belongs to
the evolving patterns of creation, how "He never reveals
Himself in the same form twice." Creation is not a static
expression of the divine, but a continually changing
panorama that embodies the divine. As the Taoist masters
described in the *I Ching*, it is our understanding of these
patterns of change that allows us to participate most
creatively and harmoniously in life.

These patterns of change reflect how energy flows,
through patterns of relationship in the outer world, and
between the inner and outer world. One of the causes of
our present world predicament is that we have forgotten
these patterns of relationship—they belong to the wisdom of the feminine. We need to reawaken our natural
understanding of the way all of life relates together and
also include a new dimension, the knowing of how the

inner and outer worlds relate, how the energy of life flows from the inner to the outer.

In this unfolding panorama oneness and multiplicity reflect each other, continually revealing new aspects of the divine. The patterns of life are a part of His unfolding oneness, and unless we are rooted in the prime cause, the underlying presence of the divine, we can never fully participate in life. Without an acknowledgment of the divine we will always remain on the surface, seeing the distorted reflections of our ego-self, unaware of the miracle that is taking place around us. We will not see the patterns of creation as a whole, but only as fragments.

His oneness belongs to the secret of creation, and in our awakening global consciousness part of this secret is being revealed. Knowing the oneness of life, we can consciously participate in this aspect of the divine revelation: we can help to bring His oneness alive in the world.

ENERGIES OF THE INNER WORLDS

The inner worlds are not just places of peace and harmony. Forces here are both volatile and dangerous. This is one of the reasons that humanity has been shielded from their energies, which are filtered into the outer world in a way that is not too disruptive or dangerous. Mystics who work in the inner have to go through a rigorous training in which the soul and psyche are strengthened to withstand strange and unpredictable forces. The mystic who is "a soldier of the two worlds" has to live a balanced and responsible life in the outer world at the same time as experiencing inner shifts and the impact of unexpected energies. The mystic also needs clarity in order to differentiate what belongs to her own personal psyche and what comes from dimensions of the beyond.

Our Western conditioning sees danger as primarily arising from the external physical world, although psychology has awakened us to forces in the psyche that can be dangerous and destructive. Carl Jung revealed that the ancient world of the gods and goddesses represents energies of the archetypal world that are within us all, and the eruption of conflicts or wars can come from these primal forces.[2]

Our cultural identification of the spiritual realms as "heaven" does not prepare us for the reality of the inner planes. Heaven is just one dimension in the vastness of the inner worlds. Just as the archetypal world has powers of great beauty and healing as well as violence, the inner realms that are beyond the archetypal have forces of harmony as well as chaos. There are energies of light and darkness, and other forces that originate far in the beyond. Some of these forces impact the physical realm, while others interact only on the inner. Just as our visual range is only a small part of the whole spectrum, so most people's experience belongs to only a small part of the range of energies that surround us. However, as our consciousness expands at this time of global transition, we need to expand our awareness of the worlds in which we live.

The masters of love and their servants have been working with forces of the inner worlds for generations. They have a profound understanding of the ways of the inner worlds. Part of their knowledge will be made known and given to humanity. Humanity has to take more responsibility on many different levels. This is a part of the process of evolution. As the inner and outer worlds come closer together, the forces of the inner will impact outer life more directly and this will change our experience of life. Science and mysticism will need to work together, the ancient wisdom of the East join with the knowledge of the West. This appears to have already begun, with the bringing of Eastern spiritual traditions to the West. But most of this spiritual knowledge is within the sphere of individual spiritual development. There is another spectrum of spiritual wisdom that belongs to the well-being of the planet. Part of this wisdom is working with the energies of the inner worlds.

Of particular importance are the places where the inner energies can come directly into the outer. Here the inner energies form vortexes of power that require careful attention. Through his own inner alignment the mystic can be present in these vortexes without being unbalanced. A human being is a remarkable organism that can function on many different levels at the same time. Our inner vehicles spin at a different frequency from our physical self, and can be trained to be consciously present on the inner as well as in the outer planes. We can attune our inner self to inner energy before it comes into life. In this way we can hold the energy and bring it into life in a creative, beneficial way.

We can also deflect negative energies so that they do not interfere with this work. Just as the yogi is trained not to absorb or be influenced by negative thought-forms or emotions, a mystic can be trained to stay with the inner energy that is beneficial, the quality of light that is needed by life, and to deflect other energies that may try to interfere with this work. This requires a degree of inner focus and detachment, and also a simple commitment to the work that needs to be done. Mystics are trained to do only what is needed, not to get distracted by either the inner or the outer world. A simple story about Bâyezîd Bistâmî illustrates this focus of attention:

Bâyezîd Bistâmî, sitting at the feet of his teacher, was suddenly asked, "Bâyezîd, fetch me that book from the window."

"The window? Which window?" asked Bâyezîd.

"Why," said the master, "you have been coming here all this time and did not see the window?"

"No," replied Bâyezîd. "What have I to do with the window? When I am before you I close my eyes to everything else. I have not come to stare about."

"Since that is so," said the teacher, "go back to Bestam. Your work is completed."

Through meditation and other practices we are trained to be attentive and focused. And the mystical path takes us through stages that annihilate us to everything that could distract us. This is the process of *fanâ* that takes us to the very core of our being where we are inwardly connected with what is real. But it is not enough just to have this connection; we are trained to live it regardless of any forces that surround us. The mystic is tested in the inner and outer world. The state that follows *fanâ*, *baqâ*—permanence or abiding in God—is not a passive resting in His presence, but a dynamic state of being with God. When al-Kharqani was asked, "Who is the appropriate person to speak about *fanâ* and *baqâ*?" he answered, "That is knowledge for the one who is suspended by a silk thread from the heavens to the earth when a big cyclone comes and takes all trees, houses, and mountains and throws them in the ocean until it fills the ocean. If that cyclone is unable to move him who is hanging by the silk thread, then he is the one who can speak on *fanâ* and *baqâ*."

A NEW REVELATION OF THE DIVINE NAME

All creation has the opportunity to awaken to oneness. This present shift in global awareness is a new revelation of the divine, a new way that He reveals Himself to Himself.

The energy that can awaken life carries the genetic information that is needed to help life transform. Certain patterns inherent to the structure of life—even at the cellular level—need to change if life is to fully awaken. The information that is needed for this change has to be given to life in a precise way so that it can be absorbed and acted upon by life as a unified organism. It also needs to be given with the consciousness of the oneness of all life, so that this knowing can be awakened in the cellular structure of life. His servants can help give this consciousness directly to life. If it is gradually filtered into life, a certain potency and power will be lost and life will not fully respond.

Life will come to know it is not just an ecosystem determined by patterns of survival. The higher purpose of life is imprinted into every cell of creation, but it needs to be awakened by the spiritual consciousness of humanity. This is why our participation is so important; life depends upon humanity for its survival and transformation. The work of His servants is essential—to ensure that the awareness of its divine nature is given to the whole.

Because this shift belongs to oneness, nothing will be excluded; all of life will function on a higher level. The cellular structure of life needs to reflect the awareness of all of life as a single, self-sustaining, living organism in which human consciousness has a central function. In the experience of oneness, humanity will realize its central role within the living organism of the planet—life depends upon humanity for its survival and transformation.

The presence of the Creator connects all of creation directly together. His invisible presence is the life breath of the planet, and contains the knowing of oneness. This is why a conscious awareness of our relationship to the divine is the greatest gift we can give to life, and why the return of the sacred is so vital to life. Our conscious recognition of the presence of the divine within all life allows life to realize its higher purpose. Without this note of awareness there are only the physical patterns of survival and the fragmented images of life's multiplicity. With this note life is harmonized at all levels.

In this new revelation of the divine, the consciousness of humanity plays a central role. We are the "eyes and ears of God"; through our consciousness He sees His world. As our consciousness is awakened to oneness, His oneness is reflected throughout creation. The consciousness of the whole of humanity can witness His oneness, know this divine quality. Through this knowing, His divine nature can become more fully present in His world.

Knowledge and energy are needed to help this happen. In the dimension of oneness the knowledge and the energy are one. Through His servants the energy is given to humanity, and through humanity to the whole of life. The container for this work has been created. His servants are positioned at the places of power, waiting to be used. In the reality of oneness the groups of His servants are the places of power. In them the "two seas meet," the inner and outer worlds come together. This is the place of direct revelation, imaged by the Sufi figure of Khidr. Here the inner can come directly into the outer without distortion.

The places of power have an important function in this work, as through them the energy that is needed to align life can flow directly from its source in the inner.

There is a timing to this work that is very specific, determined by outer and inner events. Mystics, present in both the unseen and the visible worlds, holding both the light and the darkness, watch the currents of energy that flow in the inner and outer worlds. There is a moment when the worlds can come together with an optimum effect for the whole of humanity. This is the moment that mystics are waiting for. It can be the moment of a global awakening, when the heart of the world starts to spin with a new energy.

The relationship between certain spiritual groups is crucial because no one group or individual holds the key to this unfolding. It can only happen through cocreative relationships. It is the bringing together of certain energies that will awaken the world. Each group that is positioned at a place of power has access to a particular vibration of energy, and when the different energies flow between these groups, a harmonic resonance can occur that is more potent than any individual energy.

Part of the awakening of the world is caused by these energies coming together in a new way and the patterns of relationships that are formed when they come together. Together we are creating the energy structures of the future, the archetypal patterns or riverbeds through which life will flow. Through us the structure of life will recreate itself, will reform along a different axis.

The new axis that is being given to life is the consciousness of oneness. At its core is a new revelation of the divine name, of the word that is God. At the beginning of each age a new divine name is given to humanity. This name is the sacred connection between the Creator and the creation. It contains in essence the esoteric knowledge that belongs to the era. The vibration of the name is the higher consciousness that defines the era. The new name that is being given can only be found in the midst of life, at the center of the world. When it is given to humanity, all of life will rejoice.

The energy and instructions that are needed for this work are being given to His servants. They are being reflected into our consciousness from a higher level, from the center of light that is the consciousness of the whole of humanity. This center exists outside of time and space, in a dimension beyond even the planes of non-being. This spinning center of light is the dimension of "In the beginning was the Word and the Word was with God and the Word was God."[3] Here the divine imprint that is behind creation is formed.

The word of God is the imprint of the Absolute, of That which has no name. The word of God is the purpose of humanity on its highest level, the divine imprint becoming known to Itself. Through the word, that which is unknowable makes Itself known. This is the beginning of revelation.

THE FOUNDATIONS OF LIFE

If the people of the world were wise enough
to plant the root of their lives
deep within the Subtle Origin
then the worldly affairs of life
would coherently follow their natural course
and harmony would abound of its own accord....
Then the peaceful order of the universe prevails
and unity manifests again of its own accord.

Lao Tzu[1]

REALIGNING THE FOUNDATIONS OF LIFE

At the beginning of a new era the foundations of life change. All of life is affected. Without such a fundamental shift, life would not evolve and recreate itself as it needs. Life would remain in patterns of the previous era and slowly die.

The present evolutionary shift is more than a two-thousand-year cycle. The awakening of the earth belongs to a multi-millennia cycle. Many different eras are converging at this present time, creating the potential for a multidimensional shift. This is why the tensions in the inner and outer worlds are so extreme.

The fact that we stand on the brink of destroying our own ecosystem bleakly states the extreme nature of our times. But if we witness this predicament from outside the dimension of cause and effect, we can see it as a statement that we have come to the end of many eras, and can recognize an opportunity for something new. Not only will our whole relationship to life and the planet change as we take real responsibility for our guardianship, but the planet itself will change. The foundations of life will shift into a higher frequency.

What is our participation in this process? How can we help life change and adapt? Humanity has a quality of consciousness that is divine. Life needs this consciousness to make the next step in its evolution. If we interact with life with this consciousness, life itself will awaken to its own divinity, a characteristic of the coming era. If we reclaim our real relationship with creation, we will give life our divine heritage, our relationship with God. Then life can realign itself with its Creator.

Humanity as a whole has forgotten that it carries this divine spark, just as it has forgotten that the world belongs to God and is a reflection of His oneness. Our collective forgetfulness stands in the way of our direct participation in life. Just as we have forgotten our divine nature, we have forgotten the real nature of life. Collectively we are unable to make this contribution; we can only participate in the shadowlands of our distorted image of life and the world.

However, there is another way to give our divine spark directly to the whole of life. This can be done by a few of His servants working together. They can help the world remember that it belongs to God, and begin the work of realigning its foundations. In order to do this work they need to have access to the places of power within the energy structure of the planet. Otherwise there will not be enough energy to make this shift.

But many of these places of power are in the midst of places of worldly power and thus covered over by the density of forgetfulness and greed. These negative forces cannot be ignored. They may be built upon illusions, but they carry the light of human consciousness, a consciousness that has been distorted to serve only the ego, but still retains its divine light. Without this light even the illusions of the world would fade away.

His servants are already present at these places of power. They have direct access to the divine within their hearts. They know how the energy structure of life needs to change. But they are waiting for another energy to be given—energy that cannot come from life's present spectrum. It is an altogether different kind of light and energy coming from beyond the play of opposites that has dominated our planet for the past centuries.

THE GIFT OF GRACE

Once we understand the primal oneness of all of creation, we realize that simply to change our attitude towards life and the ecosystem is not enough. That change just continues the illusion of separation and of our dominance over the planet. It does not reflect how the planet is an interdependent living entity. In fact, the inner life of the planet needs to change, and this change does not depend solely upon our own attitudes.

That we need to change our attitudes and behavior is apparent, but this is just part of a shift in the whole of creation. Freeing the world of pollutants and weapons of mass destruction without freeing the inner structure of life from certain negative energies will be an idealistic waste of time. In the dynamics of oneness nothing should be excluded. When we recognize the multidimensional nature of creation, we will understand how this shift has to take place on all levels. Otherwise our shift will just constellate a new imbalance.

We have lost the knowledge and tools needed to work with the energies of the inner structure of the planet. However, if the inner structure of the planet makes a fundamental shift, life can purify itself on the inner and outer planes. For this to happen, an infusion of an energy from beyond our present spectrum is needed. A new energy of awakening needs to be given to creation as a whole.

The gift of grace is always needed for transformation—we know this in our own journey. We come to a place where our own efforts and intentions cannot help us. And so we wait for the grace that is given through spiritual transmission, or through a divine intermediary like the Sufi figure of Khidr.

One of the central purposes of any spiritual lineage is to make energy available to those who are ready to receive it, who have done the required work of purification and preparation and are able to take the next step on the path. Without the gift of this energy there can be no real transformation. This energy is always a gift from a higher level; otherwise we would remain on the same level as before and there would be no real transformation. We may climb up the mountain with all our effort and attention, but the only real step is when a hand comes from above and pulls us up. However it may appear, this final step does not depend upon our effort. It is always grace.

Spiritual lineages are the guardians of the grace given through transmission from teacher to teacher. In Sufism this is the "golden chain," the uninterrupted chain of succession that stretches from the present *sheikh* of the order back to the Prophet. There are also some enlightened masters and friends of God present in the world who have direct access to this divine energy. Often they are hidden, sometimes known as the "veiled ones."[2] There is now a certain work in the world that can only be done by those who carry this transmission. This work includes bringing the energy of transmission directly into the living structure of the earth and so changing its vibrational frequency. When the inner structure of the earth spins at a higher frequency, it can free itself of many of the patterns that pollute it in the inner and outer worlds.

The difficulty of bringing this higher energy into life and into the structure of the planet is the density and the patterns of resistance within life and within our collective consciousness. Normally the energy of transformation is given to individuals who have purified themselves to a certain level and whose intention is clear. The energy can then be given directly to their higher vehicles, their spiritual energy centers. In some traditions special exercises, a purified diet, or fasting are required to prepare the physical body for the effects of a higher energy. But in our present situation the body of the earth is polluted and our collective thought-forms are self-centered. We have desecrated our inner and outer selves.

It requires extreme skill to give the energy of transformation to an individual, even when the seeker has done the work of purification and preparation. To give a similar energy to the body of the earth, to the foundations of life, with all the negative energy that is present, requires more than mastery. Certain events need to happen on the physical plane so that the world can open to the grace that is present. Then this higher energy, which is a vibration of love, can be given directly to the core of life, and the divine can become visible in a new way.

WORKING CONSCIOUSLY WITH THE UNKNOWN

Creation is waiting for an infusion of new energy. It knows its own need. Pathways have been formed in the structure of the planet to work with this energy, to enable it to flow where it is needed. These pathways link together the places of power that belong to the new era. The pathways and the places of power have their guardians to protect them, to ensure that they are not polluted or misused. These places of power are doorways of light through which love, knowledge, and meaning can be given, through which the future can reveal itself.

In our naiveté we think that the future of the planet depends upon humanity. But we are only cocreators of our collective destiny. There are other forces and influences that need to be recognized and included. The planet itself has its own agenda, and there are also forces that come from the beyond. We need to acknowledge that we are a part of an interdependent living organism that contains many different relationships. We have begun to recognize the complexity of our physical ecosystem. When we begin to see how our ecosystem functions on many different levels—in both the visible and invisible spectrum—we will glimpse the vastness of our world.

Part of our limitation is that we have created a God who fits into our world, rather than acknowledging a divine presence who is beyond our understanding and imaginings. When we say we look towards God, we are often looking towards an image we have created ourselves, a personalized figure, usually caring and beneficial. We filter the energies of the beyond through this image we have created, discarding what does not appear to fit into our personification. In this way we deny ourselves a real relationship with the divine and its unlimited potential. We also fail to recognize the part that we are playing in denying His indefinable presence.

If we can leave behind our images of the divine and accept the truth that "no one knows god but God," we allow the vast and unknowable to interact with us more fully. We do not limit the divine by our own preconceptions and are open to participate with a wider spectrum of divine energy. The mystic who is immersed in unknowing is a servant of a Beloved whose face is always hidden, whose ways are beyond her comprehension.

The inner surrender of the mystic has a quality that is not passive but is a dynamic participation with the unknown. We surrender to a reality we cannot understand, and are trained to stand in the midst of the emptiness and be available for His work. The moment we define the purpose of the unknown, we limit it. So with humility, we bow down before the unknowable. This act of supplication allows the divine to come into us more fully and participate with us more directly.

The mystic is trained to work with the unknown. We follow the path of Khidr which Moses could not follow, because, as Khidr warned Moses, "how can you bear with that which is beyond your knowledge?" Khidr's actions belong to the will of God. We are asked to step outside of the parameters of our own knowing in order to embrace a vaster reality. We include this unknown in our daily life, welcoming the signs it leaves of its presence. We learn to recognize and follow these signs, weaving this other reality into our consciousness. And yet even as we welcome the unknown, we also learn to discriminate, hoping to avoid being caught in spiritual fantasies or other illusions. We work with the unknown with the wisdom of common sense.

Most mystics regard this work as part of their own individual journey through life. But nothing is separate from the whole, and in welcoming the invisible and working with its energy, we are responding to a need that belongs to all of creation. We are part of an interconnected network of light that is working with forces beyond the physical and we are a part of the vast spectrum of creation. As we welcome the unknown into our own life, we are welcoming it into all of life.

We are also recognizing the need for another reality to participate directly in life. We may call this reality "the divine," but this is just a word for energies that are beyond our comprehension. The divine has an infinite spectrum of qualities and attributes, only a few of which belong to our frame of reference. But there is a way to work cocreatively with what we do not consciously understand. There is a way to be here for His sake, even though we do not know what is being asked.

What is a fundamental example of this work? When we say a *mantra*, or repeat the name of God, we welcome the unknown, the invisible face of God, with every breath, allowing forces that belong to His invisible presence to change life. Repeating His name helps set up an energy field in which the basic sustenance of life, *prana*, is aligned with our divine nature. When we meditate, we give ourself in silence to what is beyond our mind and ego; we allow His unknowable qualities into ourself and our life. And when we live with a simple awareness of the presence of the divine, knowing that all life is sacred, we witness His hidden face. The effects of such practices are immeasurable.

When we consciously welcome the presence of the unseen, the unknowable, we enable aspects of His invisible presence to affect life. We stand between the worlds and welcome what we do not know or understand, and in our surrender we consciously participate in bringing these energies into creation. Without our conscious attunement to this work, these energies would lack the spark of consciousness and could enter life only at an unconscious level. Then they would have to find their way through the debris of our unconscious selves, which takes longer and is less effective. Our consciousness is like a clear light that can guide these energies where they are needed. Consciousness gives these energies a more direct access to the energy structure of life.

A VIBRATION OF LOVE

The energies of the beyond can come into life through the participation of mystics who are trained to work with them. Mystics are linked through a network of light so that they can work together—their Higher Selves are in harmony and each is inwardly attuned to this network. The simplicity of this structure enables the energy to flow freely into life. The aspect of the mystic that is present in the unknown welcomes energies from the beyond, while the part that is present in the outer world brings these energies into life. One face of the mystic looks to the Creator, while another looks to the creation.

These energies, these qualities of the divine, are waiting to be used. They are between the worlds where they have the most direct access to the energy structure of life. Life is waiting for them. And His servants are prepared; they have been positioned where they are needed. Their hearts are aligned with the higher purpose of life, which needs this energy to come alive. The forces of darkness are also present, trying to exclude anything that would interfere with their desire for dominance.

Yet an essential ingredient is currently missing. The vibration of love that will come with the energy of awakening is not present. This love, which is passed through living spiritual lineages, has yet to be given. Without this vibration of love, the energy of awakening will not resonate with the new way the divine is revealing itself. The foundations of life will not shift to a new axis.

This note of love can constellate the energies from the beyond in a way that will enable their full potential to be used for our unified development. Nothing can fully transform without it. This love can harmonize these energies with the needs of the present time, needs which include all of creation. Without this note of love, the energies that are being given could remain just on the surface of life, rather than penetrating to the core, to the foundations of life.

Part of the training of the mystic is to be patient and to be present without wanting anything. This practice of spiritual poverty allows us to wait for the will of our Beloved without interfering. And in this waiting we hold open the pathways of light; we stand at the vortexes of power, knowing in our hearts that only His will can transform the world. And yet in this waiting there is also an expectation, because we have seen what can be given to humanity; we have glimpsed the future that is being born. We hold this knowledge for humanity, for those who are too caught up in their own affairs to see the light of this dawn.

We also sense the power that is waiting to be used, the power that belongs to God. As the dramas of worldly power play out upon the outer stage, we know how His omnipotence can come into the world. And holding this awareness, we prepare ourselves for the next stage of the work, when the invisible will become visible, when what is real will become known. It is the work of the mystic to act as midwife in this inner change.

At this time of transition more help is available than people know. Light and love are present. While the frequency of the love that is present is not that of the love that will be given with the energy of awakening, it is of great value as we prepare for the changes around us. It can help align us with what is higher in ourselves and in the world, and help us receive what is being given. But we need to learn to work with light and love, to recognize that love is not limited to our human relationships, not constrained by our own desires. Rather, love has a dimension that comes from the beyond, from a place of pure oneness and light. That love and light will separate what is true from what is false. It will bleakly reveal the corruption that is hidden in our midst.

We have been deceived too long, have given away our birthright as divine beings for a few pieces of silver. We have been convinced that we are not eternal beings, but are only here for a few years of self-indulgence. And no one has told us the real cost of our actions.

What will happen to humanity when people realize how they have been cheated? How will they respond when they recognize the depths of their own self-indulgence? And can we blame anything except our own ignorance, our own desire to escape the light? But this era of degradation is coming to an end. Our collaboration has its consequences; so much of the beauty of the inner and outer world has been destroyed; so many truths have been lost. As we take responsibility for ourselves and our planet, we will be faced with what we have done. We cannot welcome in the dawn without seeing the scarred landscape we have created. His love will show all this to us.

THE NAME OF GOD WITHIN CREATION

In every era new truths are revealed; a new way of praising and knowing God becomes possible. Just as we await a higher vibration of love, so too do we await a higher vibration of consciousness that will be given. Love and logos are the feminine and masculine dimensions of the divine, and in the future both will be revealed anew. The new revelation of the logos, the new name of God, is a vibration that will help all life give conscious recognition to its true nature. The new name of God contains the whole esoteric future of humanity. It will resonate with the higher vibration of love, and awaken human consciousness to its own divinity.

In the midst of the degradation around us, there are signs of a new beginning. Forces of unity are making their presence felt and life is responding. Just as love will show us what we have destroyed, it will also reveal underlying truths that have been hidden for centuries. These truths are coming alive, nourished by energies from the beyond. They are part of the nerve centers of the new life, the new patterns of relationship that are being formed. These truths speak to us of our eternal nature and how we can leave its imprint with every breath we take. There are truths about the relationship between the inner and outer and the inherent harmony between masculine and feminine. And there are deeper truths about the way life brings the divine into manifestation, reflecting His name in a myriad of ways. And in the understanding of these truths we will learn again to read the signs of God in the inner and outer worlds.

When we welcome His light, we acknowledge our own ignorance and wisdom. We see the crisis of our collective degradation and the wonder of divine revelation. We know that we cannot take a real step without Him, and yet we have to make this step alone, honoring our responsibility. And behind all of this is the primal truth that we are here for His sake. Every leaf and empty Coke can is a reflection of His hidden face, a way for Him to come to know Himself.

There is a magical relationship between a name and that which is named. In the original sacred languages (for example Sanskrit) the vibration of the word was also the vibration of the thing which it named. The name contained the essence of that which it named. This is reflected in the magical power attributed to names: to know the real name of an object or person allows an adept to control or manipulate the inherent structure of what is named, and thus have power over it. This magical dimension of language is used in *mantras*, incantations, and the casting of spells. It is also why in some tribal cultures a person's real name is kept secret, as to know someone's secret name is to have power over him (as for example in the tale of Rumplestiltskin). Sound and language are powerful tools.

The new name of God is being given. It belongs to the awakening consciousness of oneness and the interrelationship of all of life. It also belongs to the silence of the uncreated worlds. It is a meeting of silence and sound, formlessness and form. It has great power, power that is needed to recreate the world and shift its vibrational axis. And in the simplicity of oneness the revelation of this name is the shift in its vibrational axis, is the recreation of the world.

Without an understanding of the name of God we will only see the effects of the new era and not realize its deeper meaning. We will remain on the outside of creation rather than fully participating in its revelation and real meaning. We will not understand the sacred relationship between the name, that which is named, and the creation. In each era He gives Himself a new name and reveals the meaning of this name in creation. All of the magical secrets of creation belong to this relationship between God and His name.

Once we abandon a hierarchical image of creation and step into a new relationship of oneness within life, we will see every atom as a microcosm of the whole; every cell will reflect the new revelation of His divine name. The new revelation of His name is the next era. In order to understand the real meaning and implications of the new era, we need to understand the new name of God. This is the foundation of life.

The actual word itself is hidden, waiting to be un-covered by those who will hold it in trust for humanity. And yet it is already affecting us, awakening nerve cen-ters in the body of the earth and in the consciousness of humanity. It is speaking to us directly, reminding each of us of the unique stamp of the Creator that we carry within us. Its vibration can awaken our own unique name, the name given to us before the creation which we carry in our soul. This is the name we were given by God, which resides in the core of our heart. When this name is awakened, we come to know our unique purpose in life, the note we are here to play in life's symphony. The resonance of His name, which speaks to each of us in our own way, has the potential to dissolve the condi-tioning of the past era.

And through the magic and power of His name we will come to understand the real patterns of relationship that belong to life, not the imposed relationships that belong to the last era. We will see how we can relate together in a creative and supportive way, and also how the many different facets of creation, the many animate and inanimate forms of His world, interrelate. His name can reveal the patterns and harmony of the whole of creation.

There are those who will try to use this power and knowledge for their own ends. They will try to manipu-late the forces of creation and influence its patterns of relationship. But they cannot interfere with the unfolding of the whole. The forces of life are stronger than the constrictions of personal power. The new name of God is already being given to life and to humanity. It is present in every atom. It is subtly shifting the forces of creation, changing the energy patterns of life. It is trying to awaken us to our true nature.

Why do we not feel its presence? Why is there so much discord in our world, so many dynamics of power and suffering? Because a certain veil has not yet been removed—the dawn is still clouded by the mist. It would also be too great a shock to suddenly awake to what is real, to see the depths of our self-degradation in the bright light of what is true. And something has yet to be given to humanity and life, the secret ingredient, the vibration of love that belongs to the future. Until this is given we have to wait.

RELATIONSHIPS OF ONENESS

While we are waiting there is work to be done, preparations and connections to be made. What has been born in the silence and unknowing needs to be brought into the visible world. We need to immerse ourselves in the present where the foundations of life are being reformed, and recognize that something primal has changed deep within each of us. This shift is so simple it is easy to overlook; because it is not yet fully formed it can be dismissed as vague. But it has a fundamental message: we are the foundations of life. We carry the secrets of the whole of creation within us. The knowledge we need is not other than us.

The reality of oneness is a cornerstone of creation. The awareness of oneness and of the interdependence of life is no longer an esoteric secret but has permeated every field of life—psychology, healing, the arts, economics. But as yet we have not fully understood the potency of this realization: that every human being has conscious access to the whole of creation, and because we each have this direct access there is no need for the hierarchies of power. We each have our unique connection to the whole, and this connection is two-way: we influence the whole and the whole affects us. The more we work with the whole, the more the whole responds and works with us. This is part of the dynamics of oneness.

We are conditioned to believe that to be effective on a large scale we need to work through an organization. We overlook the simple reality of oneness: our unique oneness speaks directly to the greater oneness. If we filter this through an organization we lose our potency.

At the foundation of this relationship of oneness is the relationship of God and humanity: He who is one and alone relates to each of us directly and uniquely. He does not relate to us via an organization, through any hierarchy of power, but through our Higher Self or soul. The relationship with God is always one-to-one. This truth was repressed by the Catholic Church when they persecuted the Gnostics in order to protect their hierarchy and power, but it has always remained the most simple spiritual truth. He reveals Himself within the hearts of those who love Him, not within an organization.

We may understand how this unique relationship belongs to our inner relationship to God. But in the realm of oneness the divine is not just an inner figure but an all-encompassing reality which embraces everything. Our relationship with God includes economics and global politics as well as prayer. In whatever way we relate to the divine, whether in the inner or outer world, it is one-to-one.

And this oneness is not just a spiritual ideal but a practical reality which functions through the organic wholeness of creation in which every part relates directly to the whole. Learning to work with this oneness will liberate us from many of the patterns of our present civilization that constrict our natural way, and open us to more efficient and dynamic patterns of life. At the basis of these new patterns will be the unique relationships of each part to every other part and to the whole. And the beauty of these patterns is that they will be self-organizing. They will not be imposed but will come from the energy of life itself which will give them both strength and flexibility. They will not be crystallized patterns whose rigidity requires force to implement, but fluid and continually responsive to the changing needs of the moment.

The new patterns of life are already present in the inner planes. But they need our conscious participation to bring them into the outer flow of events. These patterns will reflect back to us a natural simplicity that belongs to life as a whole. And they have a magic. Because they belong to life as it is, they carry the magic inherent in life, the magic that helps things grow and adapt. And because we do not need energy to force these patterns onto life, we will discover that we have more energy, more power and potential. Much of our present life energy and personal power is used to try to control our inner and outer nature, to repress what does not fit into our manufactured culture. The future can bring a deep release of life force, creativity, and pure joy.

The shadow will also be present, forces that will want to manipulate the new patterns, control what is being given freely. They will be deceptive and cunning, playing to our greed and other weaknesses. We are not evolving towards purity or perfection, but towards a living of oneness in which dark and light coexist. But there will be a way to work with the shadows of the future that involves not domination but acceptance and understanding. We will need not to deny our darker self but to work to be conscious of its deceptions. We will see that the darkness is necessary, that it has an energy we need. No longer dominated by the ideologies of duality which need to imprison what they cannot control, we will understand that there are ways for us to include the darkness without being endangered. This will require a greater degree of responsibility and self-awareness than belongs to our present collective, but life itself has a wisdom it will teach us.

THE POSSIBILITIES OF LIFE

These ideas belong to the blueprint of the future, the possibilities inherent in life. How the patterns within life manifest and whether these ideas come to fruition depends upon a number of factors. One factor is the participation of individuals awakened to these possibilities. Even the simple awareness of these possibilities brings the spark of individual consciousness into the flow of new life. And with this awareness we will be able to consciously participate in this birth. The moment of transition from the inner to the outer, before the forms of the outer constellate, is crucial to the future. As the energy comes from within, it can be aligned with the possibilities of life that are most beneficial to the whole. We carry these possibilities within our consciousness; they belong to the seeds of the future which we have been given.

The places of power are of great importance, because here the most potent forces of life are coming into being. Here are many of the deciding factors of the future. And here there could also be a battle for control of this energy. Will it be given to the whole of humanity in service to what is real, or will it be constellated once again in the hands of a few? Because the places of power are not hidden in remote locations, but in the marketplace of our world, they can be open to anyone who has a direct access to the inner. And yet, paradoxically, it is this openness that protects them—they are hidden in the light rather than the darkness.

There is a rhythm to this time of transition that carries the beat of this coming era. If we can attune ourselves to it, we will be a part of the new life as it happens. We will have pushed aside the dynamics of separation to participate as a part of the flow. We are the life that is being born. The simplicity and directness of this energy of life take us into the space that has already been created, where life can reveal its primal unity and its knowing of itself.

The foundations of life have already shifted; the patterns of creation are in the process of being reformed. In this time of transition, forces from the unknown will permeate our life with both danger and opportunity. There is need for extreme attentiveness.

And yet all is according to His will because it is He who is recreating Himself, revealing Himself in a different way. We are a part of this recreation, but in the infinite spectrum of His visible and invisible Self we are only a very small part. The nature of the ego is to place itself at the center of the stage, in the starring role. The Self knows a different stage with many other actors, some visible and many hidden. And through this drama His story is told again and again. As His unchangeable Self changes, so life changes. And we are part of His unchangeable nature and His changing appearance.

A new chapter in the book of life is being written. It will affect each of us more than we can imagine. It will bring into our life energies of the inner world that until now have been hidden. And soon a new vibration of love will be born, a new way for His presence to become known. The foundations of life are being aligned with this vibration of love, this new revelation. It will give each of us the opportunity to come closer to who we are, to be present in life as our real self. And then the world can come into balance:

> Let all people return to their true nature....
> Then, once again
>   people will regain the natural virtue of wholeness.
> The world will be naturally ordered.[3]

THE LANGUAGE OF LOVE

Light the flame of your soul with the light of love
From the Beloved learn the hymn of love
Like the strings of the lute, sing the secret of secrets
Like the nightingale untie the story of the
mysteries.

Attâr[1]

LIFE AS AN EXPRESSION OF DIVINE LOVE

In the heart of the world the future is being written in the language of love. Our ability to read this language will determine whether we participate creatively in our own destiny and the destiny of the world or whether we are victims of fate, blindly reacting to the events that happen to us.

All of creation is a manifestation of divine love; every atom spins on an axis of love, and every form from a butterfly to a bomb is an expression of a quality of love. Through our understanding of the primal language of how love manifests in creation, we can help to guide the world through the changes that are taking place; we can work with the ways He is revealing Himself to Himself.

How we interact with life is crucial. Our relationship to life determines the way the patterns of events constellate around us. Our understanding of the changes taking place affects the nature of these changes, and helps determine whether they carry a quality of consciousness or remain in the cycle of unconsciousness. What is conscious can evolve at a higher frequency than what remains unconscious. In consciousness there are possibilities that do not exist at an unconscious level—for example, communication with each other and with God. If we can read the language of love, we can consciously participate in His unfolding creation.

The language of love is how we interact with life. But we have forgotten how to read the signs of life and we have relegated the language of love to our images of romance and personal relationships. We need to return to the primal recognition that creation is an expression of divine love. Even in the times of suffering His love is being revealed.

Many spiritual paths help us access love, particularly at times of suffering, and help us understand the language of love, the ways the Beloved is trying to speak to us. How we respond to the suffering in our individual life, whether we contract and close ourself off or open ourself to the meaning of the experience, determines whether we can access the love that is hidden within the experience. Spiritual paths point us beyond the plane of action and reaction to a deeper response to life. Through practices of loving-kindness we try to participate in life from the perspective of love, while the journey of individuation guides us beneath the surface of our suffering and our patterns of reaction to remain open to love and its ways of expression.

But as a new vibration of love comes into being, the ways of love will change. The language of love will be written in a different way. Many images of meaning have been burned, destroyed, desecrated. The images and symbols, which help to sustain the world, will need to be recreated, and we can take part in their creation in ways that previously were not accessible. We can help write the book of life in ways that in the past have been known only by initiates. This is because we are being given access to the places between the worlds where the formless comes into form, where the images of creation are constellated. Once we know how to read the language of love, we can begin to understand the patterns of creation, the way His love comes into form.

In the Sufi tradition there are texts on the mystical language of love. Sufi writing, particularly its poetry, is a map of the ways of divine love, helping the wayfarer to understand this bewildering journey that takes us back to our Beloved. For example, there is a detailed esoteric symbolism of the parts of a woman's body, how each part suggests a different expression of divine love.[2] In this symbolism the eye is the quality of the mystery of God's vision, the inner vision of the Beloved, while the mole or beauty spot signifies the Divine Essence itself, the pivot of all motion:

> The Wheel of Heaven turns
> > about that beauty spot
> > > like a compass rapt in reverie.[3]

The Beloved's sweet lips signify the Divine Word and Her ruby lips represent the esoteric dimension of the "Word." Her curls or tresses symbolize the hidden recesses of Divine Selfhood, the tresses' twine symbolizes Divine Mysteries, and the ringlet is the difficulties of the world of multiplicity, which cause particular anguish for the beginner on the path:

> By the fragrant breeze from your tresses' ringlet
> > I am forever drunk;
> While the dissembling guile of your bewitching eye
> > Devastates me at every breath.[4]

Through this symbolic language the poet describes the ways of his Beloved, the many aspects of divine love. He uses images of feminine beauty to speak about the esoteric nature of the divine and the mystery of the soul's experience of divine love. Although these images are of a woman's physical body, they describe His metaphysical nature. The beloved who is being described is not a beautiful woman but an inner, invisible lover.[5] The hidden beauty of a veiled woman is used as a metaphor for the hidden beauty of a Beloved who veils Himself from us, revealing Himself only in secret moments of mystical ecstasy or inner vision. In fact this inner love affair often involved renunciation of the sensual world.[6] These texts and their detailed symbolism may help us to understand the inner aspects of divine love, how His unmanifest nature has different qualities and how we experience these qualities. But they belong to a time when the emphasis was on love's unmanifest nature, and the outer world of the senses was seen as a place of difficulty that distracted the wayfarer from the real work of the path.

As the cycles of revelation change, we are now being drawn to understand the language of love as it manifests in outer life, how the patterns of creation reflect His love. It is no longer enough to look inward and experience the unmanifest qualities of the divine. We need to rediscover the language of love which belongs to the outer world. Our work is to learn anew the mysteries of His revelation, how the many qualities of His love are expressed in the outer world, and how love links the inner and outer, the unmanifest and manifest worlds.

DOORWAYS OF LIGHT

At its deepest level the language of life is the language of His love for us and our love for Him, the wonder of "He loves them and they love Him." Everything in creation witnesses Him, and human beings have the capacity to consciously incarnate the love that is at the core of this witnessing. Our remembrance of Him in His creation is an act of love. We remember Him because we love Him.

In this love all the patterns of creation are present in essence, just as the love for God contains within it the love for all aspects of His creation. The One is the many, just as the many is a reflection of the One. In order to learn the language of His love for us as it is manifest in creation, we need to realize the oneness that embraces everything and that also reflects the uniqueness of every facet of creation. In this oneness the patterns of life that are the language of love can become visible.

How can we learn the language of His love? Being present within His creation is the first step. This does not mean just to be present in life, but to be present in *His life*. Only when we recognize that it is His life that we are witnessing can we be receptive to what He is telling us. Otherwise we will just see the distorted reflections of our own self and its struggles. But when we open our eyes to witnessing Him, we can begin to learn the language that is His love. Just as in our inner relationship with the Beloved we learn to be silent and receptive to His voice, we have to let life speak to us. We need to recognize that life is a constant communion between lover and Beloved. Each moment He is revealing Himself in a new way, speaking to us in a thousand voices, which are also one voice.

This revelation does not take place just in a "spiritual mode," amidst the beauty of nature, in the inspiration of uplifting music, or in silent places of reflection. Everything is included in this revelation, in this dialogue of love: the noise of traffic on the freeways, the crowded supermarket, the multi-channel television.

His love has so many forms, from the smallest hummingbird to our weapons of war. What matters is that we recognize the stamp of His oneness and the texture of His love. Then we can participate in the creative dialogue with life that is a dialogue with our Beloved. Through this dialogue we can learn about His world, which is where we live and breathe and work and play. Then amidst the debris of our present ego-centered world we will see a very different landscape full of wonder and magic. The veil of separation that has created our world of hunger amid plenty, of poverty and soullessness, will lift and we will realize that we were always present in another dimension where His light is more visible.

Once we are present within His world, doorways of light will open. These doorways have always been among us, visible only to initiates. But as the worlds are coming together, these doorways of light will be more accessible, their energy more available. In the light that comes through them we will be able to see more clearly, understand more directly. "In Thy light shall we see light."

We need His light in order to read the book of life, the book that contains the deeper purpose of creation and our role in its purpose. In the shadows and distortions of our worldly vision we cannot read this book. The book of life is not a static book but a fluid, constantly changing, multi-layered play of energy. We cannot grasp it with the rational mind, only with a heart awakened to the knowing of love and in the light that is given.

In the book of life we can see the energy patterns of creation, the rivers of light that flow between the worlds. We can see how the individual relates to the whole and learn the secret ways to bring light into the world; we can understand the deeper purpose of the darkness and suffering in the world, of its seeming chaos. And the attentive reader can glimpse another reality behind all of the moving images of life, a reality that is alive with another meaning in which our individual planet has a part to play in the magic of the galaxy. Just as there are inner worlds, each deeper and more enduring, there are also different outer dimensions whose purposes are interrelated and yet different. The inner and outer mirror each other in complex and beautiful ways, and in this mirroring there are also levels of meaning. As we awaken from our sleep of separation, we can come alive in a multifaceted, multidimensional universe that expresses the infinite nature of the Beloved.

THE COMMUNION OF THE SOUL AND LIFE

Love has a knowing of its source. Because the nature of love is oneness, through love the creation and the Creator celebrate their essential unity, and the lover has the capacity to be conscious of this unity. She can become conscious of the real nature of our relationship with what is behind the façade of creation. In the midst of life this relationship is being constantly revealed, but we have forgotten to read the signs of revelation just as we have forgotten the relationship between the created world and God. When we reestablish this relationship in the collective consciousness of humanity, our wounds will be healed, our forgetfulness banished. It is the work of those in service to love to reestablish this relationship that is the axis of the world.

How do we do this work? How can we bring our knowing of God into the collective? The book of life has the knowledge we need, of the ways of love that belong to all aspects of life. And this book is all around us because it is our relationship to life—not our *imagined* relationship but our *real* relationship. The book of life is the communion of our soul and life, and its meaning is expressed in the language of love. Love is the language of what is real in this world, not our conditioned responses and reactions, the patterns of our projections. Love touches on all aspects of our life and reveals their essential nature. The essential nature of our life is our constant communion with God, with the unnamable source of everything that exists.

These may seem like just spiritual ideas divorced from the daily demands that surround us. But they are the foundation of what is real in our life, and our ability to reconnect with this foundation determines whether our life is meaningful, has purpose beyond the gratification of the ego. There is also a simplicity to reconnecting with our essential nature and living this connection. Each moment life is trying to tell us about what is real, speak to us in ways that we can understand. Just as through being receptive and attentive we can learn the language of our dreams, with a similar attitude we can learn to read the book of life as it is happening around us, as He is revealing Himself moment by moment.

In personal relationships we discover how, through being open and vulnerable, our heart can speak to us and to our partner, how there are deeper levels of communication than just words or touch. Life is also a relationship founded upon love—"I was a hidden treasure and I longed to be loved, so I created the world." Through an openness of heart we can participate in this relationship of love that is around us every moment of every day. And just as in a human relationship, there will be times when we feel misunderstood, unappreciated, even rejected by life. But this is part of the ways of love that belong to life. Love is not just acceptance and understanding, softness and warmth. Love also has a cruel face and a sharp sword. Love knows pain and rejection as well as tenderness.

But it is important that we bring our heart into life just as we would into any relationship of love. Through the heart we have the most direct access to the language of love with which the book of life is written. Through the heart we can glimpse the deeper secrets of life, have access to the doorways of light that can help us to read what is written. Gradually we can learn to see this language as it is written all around us, not just in rare moments of illumination.

Life needs us to read its story, to bring its hidden meaning into the light of consciousness. We carry the consciousness of life but have been using this conscious-ness for our own sake rather than for the sake of the whole of life. Without our consciousness the story of life cannot be known—we would have "had the experience but missed the meaning."

THE BOOK OF LIFE

How can we read the book of life, how can we awake to the language of the heart? Once we realize that ev-erything is a mirror for His face, an expression of His oneness, we are aligned with what is real within life. And life will speak to us, each in our own way, according to our own nature.

There are an infinite number of ways that love comes into the world, and we should not deny any of His expressions of Himself. For centuries we have been denying the aspects of life that do not appear to fit into our model of what is spiritual, our interpretation of His ways. We have tried to condition God according to our conceptions, splitting Him into a duality of spirit and matter, light and dark, masculine and feminine. But in the depths of the heart there is no duality, just an expanding knowing of oneness. Life is an expression of His all-inclusive nature. By looking at the myriad of forms—the rat eating refuse, the lily opening its petals—we are shown reflections of a God who does not limit Himself, who does not fit into our moral categories. If we are to read the book of life, we have to open ourself to His ways of expression in which the deepest sorrow can be the knowing of His love.

In the midst of life's multiplicity there is a single theme, the theme of His love for us. This is the thread that runs throughout creation. When we align our heart with this thread, we can see how it is woven into so many forms, how it has so many manifestations. Once we step outside the prison of our preconceptions and allow the love within life to speak to us, to tell us its own story, we will find a very different world that is continually coming into being around us.

Do we dare to leave behind the conceptions of duality with their many judgments and become open to a universe of beauty and violence that is neither safe nor understandable? Can we step outside the bunkers of our conditioning into the world as it is? Inside are the images of a culture that tries to reject what it cannot control. Outside in the wilderness His story is being told, His love revealed according to His ways.

To read the book of life requires courage and craziness. Slowly or suddenly you are drawn into its pages; you realize that you are part of a story vaster than you could imagine. Here there are no boundaries of success or failure, but an interrelated world in which nothing is separate, in which every action, every thought, every prayer affects the whole on many different levels.[7] And all of this tapestry is held together by love. Without love the images of life would dissolve and its substance fade away.

And this love is a part of us. When we open our heart to life we actively participate in the flow of love—love that is not just a feeling, but a dynamic energy that carries the consciousness of its Creator. Like two lovers meeting, the love within our heart merges with the love within the world. And in this meeting we realize that it is the same love: we are a part of the same oneness flowing into different forms and yet remaining one. Love shows us the illusion of separation and reveals the meaning of the interconnectedness that is all around us. Love can show us the patterns within life and what they mean. As love flows from form to form it leaves a trace of its source, a trace we can see with the eye of the heart. This trace is the meaning of His love, the underlying purpose of life. When we recognize it, we become awake and directly participate in life's knowing of itself.

Without our participation, part of the book of life is not read, its beauty not seen. Life needs the participation of mystical consciousness so that its secrets can become known, so that it can reveal itself to itself more fully. Life is asking for us to drop our illusion of separation and with an open heart to step into its oneness. When our heart is open, we can commune with life at the level of His love. In this communion of love qualities of life can become known that otherwise would remain hidden. Through the heart we can see the names of God as they are written in creation.[8] By knowing and understanding the names of God, we can have access to the magical nature of life, to its power and beauty.

The names of God are not abstract divine qualities, but energies of light and power that are needed by life to sustain it. His names and attributes are part of the divine essence of life through which He reveals Himself. Ibn 'Arabî explains, "God discloses Himself to the lover in the names of engendered existence and in His Most Beautiful Names."[9] Uncovering the divine names is part of the journey of the mystic back to God. It is also part of His revelation of Himself. When His names are recognized, another dimension of the names is awakened. Through our conscious relationship with the divine names within creation, life's divine energy is activated— the book of life comes alive in a new way.

THE DIVINE NAMES

The mystic is in service to life as an expression of the divine. This attitude of service gives us direct access to the divine within life in a way that is shrouded from those who are driven by the desires of the ego. And life responds to the open heart of His lovers. Through the dialogue of love the divine qualities in life are revealed, their energy made available. Part of the future work of the mystic will be to learn to work with these energies, the divine names, within life.

The divine names can be considered as corresponding on a higher, or spiritual level, to the archetypes of Jungian psychology, the primal energies of life that were imaged in the ancient world as gods and goddesses. The archetypal world is the intermediary plane between the realm of the soul, the world of Mystery (*'alam al-ghayb*), and the world of the senses, the world of Visibility (*'alam al-shahadat*). The energy of creation flows from the inner worlds into the planes of manifestation: from the Absolute, through the planes of nonbeing, into the plane of the soul, which is a dimension of pure consciousness and oneness, then into the archetypal, or imaginal world, where it takes on form, before manifesting in the physical world of multiplicity.[10] In the cycle of creation the energy then returns back through the archetypal world into the realm of the soul and beyond. In the past era spiritual work has focused on the individual's ascent to the inner realm of the soul and used the divine names to help facilitate this journey.

The divine names image the qualities of the divine as they exist both within the individual and within life. From the one name, Allâh, "His greatest name which includes all the other names," come the ninety-nine names, each describing a different aspect of His divine nature. On the journey of spiritual ascent the wayfarer can use the names of God as a way of embodying and developing different divine qualities, accessing and using their energy. The divine names work within the individual, helping him to develop his spiritual nature and make the transition from the outer world of the senses to the inner dimension of the soul.

In the past centuries esoteric knowledge has been revealed about how the divine names can function within the individual. Different Sufi orders developed *dhikrs* and other practices to work with these energies. A thirteenth-century Egyptian Sufi, Ibn 'Atâ' Allâh, describes how "the names of God have particular meanings and correspondingly particular effects, some of which are appropriate for beginners and some of which can be used by advanced adepts":[11]

Recollection of the Most Beautiful Names of God comprises remedies for the diseases of hearts and tools for the wayfarers to the presence of the teacher of hidden things. Remedies are not to be used except for the diseases which that name cures. When, for example, the name "the Giver" (*al-Mu'ti*) is helpful for a particular disease of the heart, then the name "the Provider" (*al-Nafi'*) is not desirable in this case and so forth. The principle is that the heart of the one who recollects a *dhikr* which has an intelligible meaning will be influenced by that meaning...

The recollection of the divine name "the Sincere" (*al-Sadiq*) bestows upon the veiled one a sincere tongue, upon the Sufi a sincere heart, and upon the Gnostic realization.

The divine name "the Guide" (*al-Hadi*) is useful in seclusion. It is useful when there is a scattering and distraction, which it removes. One who seeks God's help but does not see the external form of the helper should know that his persistence in seeking help is what he asked for...

The divine name "the Beneficent" (*al-Muhsin*) is right for the ordinary person who wishes to attain the station of trust in God. This *dhikr* brings about intimacy and hastens illumination and is a remedy for the aspirant who is fearful of the world of majesty.

The divine name "the Knower" (*al-'Alîm*) when recited awakens from heedlessness and makes the heart present with the Lord. It teaches the people of beauty manners in meditation and the attainment of intimacy, and the people of the world of majesty are renewed in awe and fear.[12]

Sufi teachers developed practices in which the practitioner tries to imagine or be suffused by the divine qualities
while repeating the name, for example patience (*sabr*),
or sincerity (*ikhlas*). The divine names when repeated
"produce spiritual energy which are the appointed agents
(*muwakkal*) that are charged with accomplishing the
desired result. Conversely, if a person doesn't recite the
name then none of this spiritual energy is produced
which makes the attainment of the desired attribute
impossible."[13]

Sufi orders also developed more detailed practices
and *dhikrs* that combine the names of God, the breath,
and movement, sometimes reciting certain names with
the practitioner's attention on different spiritual centers
in the body. The different techniques have specific effects
on the spiritual, psychological, and physical body of the
practitioner. They are ways of using divine energy for
healing and spiritual development. These Sufi practices
are similar to Hindu and Buddhist practices of *mantra* or
seed-syllable recitation. In these practices an individual
recites one or more syllables and in doing so transforms
her consciousness in accord with the vibration and
meaning of the word.

Like the archetypes, these divine names are powerful energies that exist in the inner world. The wayfarer
needs certain energy and power for the work of inner
transformation and the divine names give us access to
this energy. Our focus on the individual journey of spiritual ascent has resulted in esoteric science developing
knowledge and techniques that use the divine names
for this purpose. Using the divine names in this way has
been an important part of our spiritual development,
but it has overlooked the function that they have in the
way the energy of life comes into manifestation. Just as

we have to expand our understanding of the language of divine love from the inner journey of the mystic to embrace all of life, so we need to expand our knowledge of the mystical science of the divine names.

The energy of the divine names is needed for spiritual work in the world. Part of the next stage of our development will be to understand how divine energies work not just within the individual but within life as a whole.[14] As the inner and outer worlds come together, the spiritual science that belonged to the inner world will be expanded to an understanding of both worlds. Techniques will be developed to work with the names of God within creation, to have access to their powerful energies within its physical body and inner energy structure, and to bring these energies into everyday life.

Shamanic traditions and some schools of esoteric magic work with the magical names within life, the real names of plants, animals, and people. The divine names describe His qualities rather than separate objects, and they function at a different frequency. They belong to the interface between the archetypal realm and the dimension of pure being, where the one divine Being begins to reveal Itself through the different divine names. They are directly part of the energy structure of life, the patterns of power that lie behind creation. Through His names we can work with these qualities of energy within life.

Traditionally it is through spiritual practices, prayer, and meditation that the mystic is given access to the divine names, their qualities and energy—they are inwardly revealed not just as words but divine qualities. Experiencing them within life may require a different approach as spiritual practices often turn our attention inward, away from life. Practices have yet to be developed that work directly with these names within life. We need to allow life to reveal its hidden nature to us, its embodiment of the divine. But first we have to leave behind any attitude that separates our inner self from outer life—an attitude of separation denies us access to these qualities.

Because the heart is the organ of divine perception and oneness, our heart needs to be open to life as it would be open to the Beloved. We have to be attentive and receptive to life as an expression of the divine. Open and vulnerable, we have to wait for the divine names to reveal themselves to us, just as we wait for the Beloved to come to us. We have to be attentive for this divine knowledge to be revealed. And it may appear differently from the way we expect. His revelation continually changes. We may be taken by surprise, tricked, and drawn beyond any of our preconceptions. He loves to deceive us, to laugh at our limitations, and draw us always deeper into His revelation of Himself.

Turning our real attention away from our individual divine qualities towards life's spiritual nature, we will see His signs within life, how His names are woven into the fabric of creation. As we learn how the energy flows from the inner to the outer world, we will use spiritual principles and techniques to work with this energy. We will come to understand how the divine names can re-align life with its higher nature, restore life to its innate harmony and balance, and help us to bring healing and beneficial energies into the midst of the outer world. Just as the shaman worked with the inner energies of life and its centers of power for the benefit of the tribe, so can the spiritual practitioner learn to use the knowledge of the divine names for the benefit of the whole.

NEW FORMS OF LOVE

The language of love and the science of the divine names will give us new ways to work creatively with the energies of life, with the way life manifests into form and how it continually changes and evolves.

Human consciousness can be aligned with the energy patterns of creation so that we can influence these patterns before they constellate into form. In this way, we can participate directly in the evolution of life, in the capacity of life to express the divine. Through the use of the divine names within creation we will have access to the magical power and potential of life. Through our understanding of the language of love we can work in harmony with the deeper purposes of divine oneness, consciously helping life to bring into being forms that reflect this harmony. For example, economic and political structures can be changed so that they are expressions of divine oneness rather than ego-centered power and greed.

We can also give birth to forms that are an expression of our higher nature, just as in the Renaissance in Italy art was used to express forms of beauty and harmony that embodied divine proportions. (This is quite different from much contemporary art which appears to reflect the distortions of the personal psyche and other aspects of contemporary life.) The new forms that are waiting to be born into life will be produced as our consciousness reflects what is higher; then we can bring it into material form.

Nature effortlessly creates forms that reflect the beauty and majesty of the Creator. But these forms change very slowly, evolving over millennia. Because of the power of consciousness, humanity has the capacity to change more quickly, to bring into being forms that reflect the changing face of the divine. We are a part of this speeded evolution and have the potential to manifest the divine in ways that are inaccessible to forces of nature. But in order to creatively participate in this dynamic of evolution, our consciousness needs to be aligned with the inner forces behind this quickened evolution. This is one of the reasons why we need to relearn the language of love and to expand our understanding of the mystical science of the divine names.

Through relearning the language of love we can read the book of life as it is written by the Creator rather than through the distortions of humanity. Through His eyes we see the patterns of His evolving oneness, the beauty and majesty through which He reveals Himself to Himself. Through the eyes of humanity we see a very different picture, dominated by the forces of our lower nature and the confusions of our mind. The language of love allows us to participate directly with His creation and its underlying oneness, rather than with our distorted perception of creation. There is a fundamental difference between the two ways of relating to life.

But the language of love requires us to give up our patterns of control. The ego has invented a world that it attempts to control. This is one of the central ideologies of our Western culture, even though it has constellated many fears and anxieties through its inability to achieve this control. The language of love is one of dynamic exchange rather than dominance or control. It is a language of relationship, our relationship with our Creator and with His world of which we are a part. The difference between relating to life through the language of love and relating to it through our present conditioning is as extreme as the difference between making love and rape. In rape there is only dominance and desecration.

The Beloved speaks most directly to us through the language of love because this is His simplest connection, the most direct expression of His essence. Love is the truth underneath all of life's manifestations, the primal note in the symphony of creation. The work of the mystic is to hold this note for humanity. Within it lies the secret of His relationship to us and to all of life.

The mystic knows how these secrets can be revealed and how life changes through this revelation. We experience this in our own life, in the ways our inner horizon expands into His infinite nature, in the ways we are drawn to experience His names and attributes. We can sense the possibilities of His revelation within life as a whole. What we have not yet fully understood is the degree of change that is possible, or how we can help this change to happen. Because the mystic lives at the very core of life, at the axis of His love for us, we have the most direct access to the energy of love as it constellates into the evolving patterns of life. The language of love can teach us how to work at this place where love comes into form, so that we can be His artists, working with His divine energies, helping to create His world.

LOVE AND LAUGHTER

What is this precious love and laughter
Budding in our hearts?
It is the glorious sound
Of a soul waking up!

Hâfiz[1]

LOVE'S PLAY OF ILLUSIONS

The need of the time pushes us to take responsibility for the planet, to uncover the secrets that are hidden within life, and to help the world awaken to a new way of being. But in the midst of this work it is important to remember that these are just signs, images of something so wonderful that it can never be named or even imagined. If we are to stay aligned with the Truth and with the real nature of love, we cannot allow ourself to be fixed in any idea, any concept, however beautiful or beneficial. We are the servants of a love that comes with a laughter that ripples through creation, always reminding us of a reality that has no form, no identity. Without the laughter of love, its trickery and mischief, it would be easy to become caught in the best of intentions and lose the essence of a Beloved who is infinite and always unknowable.

Love flows into creation from indefinable inner worlds, from the dazzling darkness where love is born. One of the qualities of love is that it moves from the formless to form, and yet remains true to its indefinable nature. Love is alive only in the moment; it is never caught, restricted. The moment you try to capture love in any pattern of identification, it has gone.

Living and working with love means to be open to continual change, to be free of patterns of restriction, the bondage of identification. We live in a world of forms, and yet His love opens us to another dimension, another way of being. In the moment of love we are with our Beloved, and He can never be restricted. He continually reveals and re-veils Himself, and in His dance of appearances His laughter is always present. Being His lover includes learning to live with His laughter and allowing ourselves to be fooled again and again, both by His dance of appearances and our inability to understand Him.

In Sufi gatherings there is always much laughter. In the laughter we lose ourself, our ideas, our preconceptions. We allow ourselves to become fools and realize the folly of our lives. Lovers know that it is all a dance, a play, and that the real meaning of life is in our relationship to the Beloved as He reveals and hides Himself. We have to catch the thread of love and meaning that is woven into His world of forms, and this means to catch the joke of love that is continually being made visible.

How can one think of this world, with its problems and sufferings, as a joke? How can one laugh about the hungry children and the world's endless cycles of violence? When one has glimpsed His tenderness and care that are present in the midst of pain and sorrow, one finds in the heart an infinite compassion for those who suffer. We see that He is "the pangs of the jealous, the pain of the sick." He is alive within these forms and yet He is beyond them. Our limitation is to be caught in the appearance. Then we lose our ability to know our Beloved and participate fully in the mystery of His revelation.

All of humanity is caught within the play of illusions. We exist within the creations of our mind and psyche, as well as within the collective patterns that define our outer life. The spiritual journey is a recognition that we are caught, and a longing to be free. To embark on this journey is to accept that we are tricked, that life is not as it appears. Through our remembrance we realize that we are continually fooled, caught in the illusions of the ego and the bewitching *maya* of life. How can we not laugh at ourself when we see how easily we are tricked, caught by our pettiness, by our desires and conditioning? And yet still we take ourself seriously, until one day His love and laughter overwhelm us.

Once the gates of grace have been opened, we glimpse another world that is real, that reflects the beauty and wonder of its Creator, in which His face is visible. And this world is around us, in the song of the bird, in the laughter of children. It is here, in every breath we breathe, and yet we cannot see with our outer eyes, only with the eye of the heart. For centuries Sufis have been His fools, seeing the world with the eyes of love, recognizing its illusions and the wonder that is His presence within this illusion.

FOOL FOR LOVE

Laughter is present within all of life, because all of life is a dance of revelation. The illusions of life, its multiplicity of desires, are a part of the way He tricks us. In the Qur'an (3:54) it is said, "The best of deceivers is Allah." Like a conjurer He seduces us with His play of images. We believe what we see with our eyes, taste with our tongue. Our religions and spiritual teachers may say, "This is not all," that "Eye hath not seen, nor ear heard, neither have entered into the heart of man, the things which God hath prepared for those that love him."[2] But how can we access this other reality that is all around us, how can we avoid being seduced by the way things appear? Can we laugh at our own seduction, knowing that it is the hand of our Beloved who makes such magic? Once we recognize that it is He who seduces us, and that this seduction is part of His revelation, then we can participate more freely in His joke.

We are continually fooled. This is part of our human condition. The mystic is the one who knows that she is fooled, and willingly allows her Beloved to trick her. She knows that this is part of His way of loving. The ascetic cuts himself away from the illusions of the world, aspiring to free himself from its grip of desires through willpower. But the lover is only concerned with her Beloved, and seeks to find Him everywhere. When we repeat His name, when we practice remembrance, we are seeking our Beloved. But even when our heart cries and we cannot find Him, when He appears absent, there is a revelation taking place. He is both "The Existent and the nonexistent ... that which is felt and that which is imagined."[3]

Nothing is as it appears. The mystic uses the image of peeling the skins of an onion to describe how we discover our true essence, and it is the same with life. Images are built upon images, revelation upon revelation. It is all an illusion and it is all He.

What is real? For the lover only the presence of her Beloved is real, and how can her Beloved ever be absent when all is He? But our experience tells us otherwise. We are tricked into experiencing a world without Him, just as we are veiled from our own divinity. God is seeking God in every breath, in every spin of every atom. We think that we are seeking God, but this is also an illusion. If all is He then the seeker is He. He is seeking Himself in the dance of His own illusion:

> By Himself He sees Himself, and by Himself He
> knows Himself. None sees Him other than He,
> and none perceives Him other than He.[4]

The wayfarer has given herself the ultimate task,
the goal of seeking God. We put all of our energy into
this quest; we suffer and aspire. And yet there is neither
goal nor seeker. There is only Oneness longing for Itself.
We are even tricked into believing that we can seek for
the Truth, that we can come closer to God. Suddenly
one day we wake up to this illusion and are filled with
laughter. We discover the final secret of the path, that
there is no secret. A friend was told this in a dream when
he was asked:

> "What is the last/greatest secret?"
> I answer but the answer comes as if something
> speaks without me interfering. "The greatest secret
> is that there is none and because of that it is kept
> the greatest secret."

Again and again the path shows how we are tricked,
deceived both by our illusions and by our Beloved. We
think that there is a path to follow, a spiritual goal to
achieve. How can we trust a path and a Beloved who trick
us so completely? But how can we not trust a Beloved
who is so complete in His trickery?

A PATH OF DECEPTION

The Sufi path is a treacherous road. If you are fortunate
you will lose everything. And the Sufi *sheikh* is the master of deceptions. Only through deceptions can we be

awakened to reality. We may begin the journey with good and serious intentions, but the *sheikh* is more concerned with the Beloved's intentions, with the way His name is stamped into our being. The work of the teacher is to reveal His name, His way of loving. And for this he needs to subvert our thinking process, seduce and ensnare us. A friend who was beginning this journey had the following dream;

> I am in a green field embracing a man. Looking up I see that the scene is being filmed. It is a scene for a movie. I leave the field and walk down a dusty road. Along the road towards me walk two men. They are well-dressed travelers. When we meet I realize that they are gamblers, father and son, and they offer to play cards with me, at twenty-five dollars a hand. I say that I will play, but only at five dollars a hand, and I want a new pack of cards. The son produces a new pack of cards from his pocket, and with the old man watching, we play one hand. I win this hand.

The dream starts with her leaving a life that is just a movie being filmed. This is the beginning of the journey, when she realizes that her life is just an illusion; she is playing a part in a movie. Then she walks down the dusty road, an ancient image of the spiritual path. On this road she meets two travelers, unaware that a traveler is a description of a mystic: "Be in this world as if you are a traveler, a passer-by, for this is not home." But these two men are not only travelers, they are also gamblers, father and son. Bahâ ad-dîn Naqshband, the founder of the Naqshbandi order, said he learnt more about the path from watching a gambler than from anyone else:

"Here was someone who was prepared to risk everything, even his head, for the next throw of the dice."

Unwittingly the dreamer has stumbled into the presence of a Sufi master and his son, with whom she agrees to play a hand of cards. Sensibly she asks for a new pack of cards, but these are master gamblers—Sufi *sheikhs* have been tricking people for centuries. They know how to deal every card, how to stack any hand. They know how to create your most precious illusion, and then by sleight of hand make it vanish or change into its opposite. In the West with our focus on science and reason we have little understanding of how such tricksters work. We become easily deceived by spiritual charlatans, by someone with a few psychic powers. But a real master can take the cards of your own life and deal them back in a new order. He confronts you with attachments that you did not know you had, and helps you lose everything you think precious. All this with a twinkle in his eye.

A master can play with the images of the world, with the patterns in your mind, with the structure of your psyche. He can free you from these illusory chains by making them appear and disappear. He is a master of the visible and invisible worlds. And he knows how to play the game of love. In the dream the wayfarer wins the first hand. This is the most basic trick of every professional gambler—you are allowed to win the first three hands, whatever is needed to get you hooked. You are given love, bliss, a state of peace, wonderful dreams. The gates of grace are opened. It is called "the honeymoon period." But then you have to pay, to pay with yourself, your values, your beliefs. By now it is too late. You are sitting at the table of love, losing every hand, being tricked again and again.

It takes courage to be fooled by love; it takes commitment to be continually tricked. The game is more dangerous than you know. But in the hands of a master gambler how can you go wrong? You can only lose. He knows every move you make. He sees your patterns of response before you act. He knows the cards you are being dealt.

In the West we tend to take ourself and our spiritual life too seriously. We color the path with the ambitions of the ego and the morality of religion. The Puritan fathers did not have much reverence for the trickster. They saw him as the devil, unlike the Native Americans who honor the coyote and the healing power of laughter. With our Puritan heritage we do not like to acknowledge that we have no control and are fooled from the very beginning. But how can we be awakened to the illusion of life except through a play of illusion?

The path plays with all of our illusions in order to free us. Again and again we are shown how we are deceived. A good teacher will continually deceive, will be a shape-changer of many forms, one who cannot be fixed in any image. He will allow the student to create an image of the teacher, and then turn it upside down. He will allow the student to hate him, to be angry, to feel cheated, betrayed. He will even play the part of a charlatan if needed. But unlike a charlatan the teacher will never have any personal gain from his actions. He is in service to love.

Behind the teacher is the laughter of the Beloved, who is the "best of deceivers." He has created a whole world of illusion that can either enslave or free us. Only His slaves, His fools, are really free. Only those who have died can really live His loving. On the path of love we give up everything, our desires, ambitions, attachments. And then we discover that this was only the beginning, only the doorway of love:

A lover was telling his Beloved
how much he loved her, how faithful
he had been, how self-sacrificing, getting up
at dawn every morning, fasting, giving up
wealth and strength and fame
all for her.

There was a fire in him.
He didn't know where it came from,
but it made him weep and melt like a candle.

"You've done well," she said, "but listen to me.
All this is the décor of love, the branches
and leaves and blossoms. You must live
at the root to be a True Lover."
                                        "Where is that!
Tell me!"
     "You've done the outward acts,
but you haven't died. You must die."

When he heard that, he lay back on the ground
laughing, and died. He opened like a rose
that drops to the ground and died laughing.

That laughter was his freedom
and his gift to the Eternal.[5]

Love and laughter open us to what always is. One of
the greatest illusions is that we are separate from God. The
Sufi path even begins with the experience of separation,
the soul's longing for God, and the promise of a journey
back to God. The images of the path capture us with the
idea of a journey back to God—the wayfarer returning
home. But if we look closer we discover that the journey

back to God is the stage of *fanâ*, the annihilation of the illusory self that leads to *baqâ*, abiding in God. For the mystic the real journey is the journey in God. After dying to ourself we awaken to the laughter of the real relationship with our Beloved.

The person who has forgotten God sees this world as real. The wayfarer is awakened to the seeming illusion of the world and makes the illusory journey back to God. But then we discover that this world is real; even if it is just an image, it is His image:

> I am both the snake and the charmer.
> I am the loosed and the bound:
> I am that which is drunk and he who gives to drink.
> I am the treasure and I am the poverty:
> I am My creation and the Creator.[6]

At this point spiritual illusions give way to spiritual reality, and this reality is filled with laughter, laughter at the way He has deceived us and at the true nature of creation. There is a joke waiting to be died for and lived. And the laughter is life itself: we are a part of His veiling and unveiling, and all around us is His revelation full of joy and mischief.

SPRING FLOWERS

What does it mean, this laughter that comes from the beyond and belongs to all of life? We struggle and suffer so much in this world of forms, often seemingly without purpose. Often we carry the pain of others, our parents, children, friends. The spiritual student is given an added burden, the longing to be free of life's illusions. We suffer the pain of separation, and confront our inner darkness. And there are often the doubts that swirl about us. Is this journey back to God real? Is it worth the pain and effort? Are we deluding ourself?

Only That which cannot be named is real. Everything else is a deception, a veil. Focused on ourself, we see the veils of suffering and effort. But if we can turn away, or step aside from ourself, a very different landscape emerges. This belongs only to the moment, and is filled with laughter. Here there is no effort or struggle, but a quality of being that is free, alive, full of joy. There is the laughter at our hubris in taking ourself so seriously, in thinking for one instant that our life was about ourself. How can something so wonderful and infinite be about something so small and illusory as our ego?

Is this self-deception just a human misunderstanding, or is it also a divine illusion? Is it our free will or His temptation that draws us into this maze? When we awaken, it seems so insignificant. But if we turn back and look into the darkness of this deception, we see our need to separate ourself from God. There is a drive within humanity to claim something for itself, to deny His overwhelming oneness, His all-pervading presence. We need to claim our own existence without Him. This drive has been at the foundation of much of Western rationalism. We have created an image of the world with man at its center, rather than the divine. And we each create an image of our own life with ourself at its center. This is so imprinted into our culture that we forget that it is quite a recent phenomenon—most earlier cultures had an image of the divine as the center of every person and every activity.

In our world of shadows, self-deception is a way of life. Without our self-deceptions our sense of self would change completely. The same is true of a good joke, whose punch line plays with our preconceptions. The joke of life is that it is really so different from any conception we may have, and once we glimpse its vaster purpose we have to laugh. We see how all of our struggles, our dramas, even our battles of light and dark, are a part of "something completely different." The laughter is an acceptance of our limitations and His wonder.

I remember when I was sixteen and a Zen *koan* first awoke me. Suddenly, inexplicably, the world was different. There was a light that I had never seen, like sunlight dancing on water. The ordinary world around me changed, and in its simplicity there was joy and laughter. This laughter was everywhere, in the trees, in people, even in my mundane studies. I would often sit in a garden that bordered a river, watching the swirl of the current and the myriad of reflections, immersed in the wonder of what is. It was as if the walls of my life had fallen away and I found myself still in the same world and yet nothing was the same. And who was laughing? It was the simple joy of real existence:

> A monk asked the Zen master Fuketsu: "Without speaking, without silence, how can you express the truth?"
>
> Fuketsu observed: "I always remember spring in southern China. The birds sing among innumerable kinds of fragrant flowers."[7]

After those few weeks the coverings of life returned, and it was many years before the laughter reawoke in me. In this laughter of life so much falls away; so many concepts dissolve as we recognize what always is. In the laughter even the search for truth seems unimportant, a memory of a quest that once held meaning. Like love, this laughter does not need to be explained. It carries its own unique quality, its own prayer and remembrance. It is His laughter alive in us.

BEING A PART OF HIS JOKE

Allowing ourself to be deceived and to laugh at the deception, we allow Him to share His secret self with us. We laugh with Him not only at our own folly and presumptions, but at what is revealed through His deception. He has created a whole universe in order to reveal Himself to Himself, and yet in every moment He says, "I am not like this." We are a part of His experience of Himself. We know Him in every touch, every taste; every experience is His experience, and yet He tells us He is beyond any sensation. In each moment He is lost and found. We can only laugh at the crazy wonder of it all.

But in this laughter something is made known. We experience an aspect of the divine that is other and yet present. The laughter takes us beyond our conceptions and yet impresses us with something alive and dynamic. In laughter there is a quality of life that is not found in serious thought or the diligence of spiritual practice. Laughter is alive with His intangible presence. We always want to confine Him in a concept or attitude, but He cannot be confined. Divine laughter breaks our patterns of conditioning and reveals His indefinable nature. Seriously we seek Him. Laughing He reveals Himself.

The danger of experiencing His deception and laughter is in not taking seriously the suffering of humanity. Logically this suffering is an illusion, but the victim of torture or abuse knows the reality of her pain and the scars it leaves. This is a part of the bondage of humanity, the price we pay for life. And those who seek God pay also with the blood of their hearts. They suffer for His sake. And this suffering is real.

How can one reconcile laughter and suffering? If there is a joke to creation, why do we suffer so much? Through the eyes of a violated child, life is no joke. We long for a beneficial God who can protect us from our pain, who can wipe away our tears and reassure us. Or a serious God who says our suffering is payment for our sins or past *karmas*. We do not want a laughing God who says it is all a joke. We need to value our suffering, protect our wounds. We do not know that we are the laughter of God, a laughter that is not conditioned by good or bad, pleasure or pain. Creation is the divine, and its joke is like a shock that reveals His hidden face.

There is no need to explain or understand. Sometimes there is sadness, sometimes joy. Living in His moment, we know the light and the darkness and something else both within and beyond the light and the darkness. Again and again we forget, and then we remember—or is it He who forgets and remembers? Is our sadness really His sadness, our joy His joy? Does it matter? We are a part of our Beloved. We cannot be other than Him, and yet He is other than us. We are loved beyond our understanding, beyond the patterns of our relative world. If we deny His laughter we limit Him, and limit our ability to live His qualities, to be in His presence. And if we live His laughter so many sensible and just ideas are lost. But it is such a wonderful joke, and we are a part of this joke, as a friend experienced:

All is illusion and dissolves in nothingness. In a great variety of images it was shown that all is illusion, fleeting, replaceable. Nothing of what we imagine exists, no good or evil, right or wrong. All disappears into a tiny opening or hole. That is all that remains of forms, dissolved in a tiny point, and not even this. And then always forms and manifestations come into being, and it is not, neither this nor that. What remains is beyond form; That, undefined, formless. At the beginning it was not so easy to follow; all was so incredibly fast, but it was so often repeated, like a kaleidoscope, here and gone, that finally it just was. Always again we try to create a form as existent. There were a lot of images (my walking path in the fields, pictures of a film, and many many more.) "This is it. So it is. This is true. This I perceive," says the mind, feelings, awareness. And then again a LAUGHTER and it is gone again. What a relief and craziness. So there is nothing that exists, that we can hold on to. And at the same time all is creating new again, makes sense for a moment, and then disappears in nothingness. What lasts: laughter, freedom, bewilderment, That? Never again I can say: "It is like this"—but probably I will do it again.

NOTES

INTRODUCTION

1. The Gospel According to Thomas 22:10, trans. A. Guillaumont, H.-Ch. Puech, G. Quispel, W. Till, and Yassah 'Abd Al Masih.

CHAPTER 1: SOURCES OF POWER

1. *Katha Upanishad, Ten Principal Upanishads*, trans. Shree Purohit Swami and W. B. Yeats, p. 34.
2. "The Hollow Men," V, *Collected Poems*, 1909-1962.

CHAPTER 2: THE POWER OF THE REAL

1. Quoted by Henry Corbin, *Creative Imagination in the Sufism of Ibn 'Arabî*, p. 174.
2. Rashahât 'Ain al-Hayât, *Beads of Dew From the Source of Life*, p. 64.
3. Rûmî, *One-Handed Basket Weaving*, trans. Coleman Barks, p. 80.

CHAPTER 3: THE LIGHT OF THE SOUL

1. *Memories, Dreams, Reflections*, p. 276.
2. In Islam this fight against the *nafs* or "lower nature" is called the *Greater Jihad*. The fight against the unbeliever is the *Lesser Jihad*.

CHAPTER 4: THE MAGIC OF LIFE

1. Quoted in the video *The Eye of the Heart: The Paintings of Cecil Collins*, Stephen Cross Productions, 1978.
2. From "All the Pockets," by Hilary Hart (unpublished).
3. See Vaughan-Lee, *Working with Oneness*, pp. 111–124, "Imagination."
4. See Vaughan-Lee, *The Signs of God*, pp. 110–117, "Reestablishing a Symbolic Consciousness."
5. Symbolic consciousness is also known as "mythological thinking." It arises from the holistic thinking process of the right side of the brain, and stands in contrast to the analytical thinking of the left hemisphere which is associated with logic and thinking in words.

"Mythological thinking" is the older process. It does not attempt to dissect or rationalize and works in images rather than in words. As opposed to the active, idea-forming process of the rational mode, it is primarily receptive, "observing the change and development of its images." It allows for the formation of symbols and so for a symbolic relationship to life.

6. E. E. Cummings, "30," "one winter afternoon," *73 poems*.

CHAPTER 5: THE ENERGY OF AWAKENING

1. Sufi prayer.
2. Jung saw the two world wars as being related to the awakening within the German psyche of the warrior god Wotan. *Collected Works*, vol. 10 , para. 371–399.
3. The Gospel According to St. John 1:1.

CHAPTER 6: THE FOUNDATIONS OF LIFE

1. *Tao Te Ching*, trans. Hua-Ching Ni, 37.
2. "Not everything in the world is meant to be visible. There are many advanced souls in the world, who live in union with God; and then there are those even further on who are named the Veiled Ones of God.... The most holy are nearly always hidden, hidden in a cloud of humility and Divine Protection." Rûmî, *Light upon Light*, trans. Andrew Harvey, p. 224.
3. *Tao Te Ching*, trans. Hua-Ching Ni, 18.

CHAPTER 7: THE LANGUAGE OF LOVE

1. *The Book of Secrets*, trans. Lynn Finegan.
2. See Javad Nurbakhsh, *Sufi Symbolism*, vol. I, for a lexicon of different symbols. The following definitions are from *Sufi Symbolism*, vol. I.
3. 'Attâr, quoted by Javad Nurbakhsh, *Sufi Symbolism*, vol. I, p. 46.
4. Hâfez, quoted by Javad Nurbakhsh, *Sufi Symbolism*, vol. I, p. 23.
5. The troubadour poets who brought this language of feminine beauty back to the West did not understand this, and so left us with the image of a beautiful and often unattainable woman, which became central to the ideals of courtly love and then part of romantic love.
6. The renunciation of the physical form of the beloved is described in the two great Sufi love stories, *Layla and Majnun* and *Yusuf and Zulaikha*.

7. To quote Lao Tzu, "...there is no isolated, single event; all events are related. There is no tree, therefore, that is separate from its root, nor any root separate from the tree. Neither can it be separated from the soil, the climate and the natural environment." "Hua Hu Ching," *The Complete Works of Lao Tzu*, trans. Hua-Ching Ni, p. 144.

8. According to Islamic Sufi tradition there are ninety-nine names of God, each name describing a divine quality or attribute, for example *Ar-Râhmân*—the All-Merciful, *Al-Musawwir*—the Shaper of Beauty, *Ad-Darr*—the Creator of the Harmful. Allâh, the Greatest Name, contains all of the divine names and attributes and is the sign of the Essence and the cause of all existence.

9. Quoted by William Chittick, *The Sufi Path of Knowledge*, p. 43.

10. For a more detailed description, see Vaughan-Lee, *Working with Oneness*, chap. 8, "Imagination," pp. 117–118.

11. Carl Ernst, *Sufism*, pp. 93–95.

12. Quoted by Ernst, *Sufism*, pp. 93–95.

13. Chisti Habibi Soofie Order: www.soofie.org.za/tasawwuf/awrad_wazaaif.html

14. This is in conjunction with humanity's gaining a fuller understanding of the archetypal world and its powerful forces and of how to work with them to benefit life.

CHAPTER 8: LOVE AND LAUGHTER

1. *The Gift*, trans. Daniel Ladinsky, p.19.

2. I Corinthians 2:9.

3. Jîlî, quoted by R. S. Bhatnagar, *Dimensions of Classical Sufi Thought*, p. 120.

4. Ibn 'Arabî, "Whoso Knoweth Himself..." from *Treatise on Being (Risale-t-ul-wujudiyya)*, p. 4.

5. Rûmî, *Delicious Laughter*, trans. Coleman Barks, p. 18.

6. Jîlî, quoted by R. S. Bhatnagar, *Dimensions of Classical Sufi Thought*, p. 120.

7. Paul Reps, *Zen Flesh, Zen Bones*, p. 138.

BIBLIOGRAPHY

Bhatnagar, R. S. *Dimensions of Classical Sufi Thought*. Delhi: Motilal Banarsidass, 1984.

Chittick, William C. *The Sufi Path of Knowledge*. Albany: State University of New York Press, 1989.

Collins, Cecil. *The Eye of the Heart*. Video. Stephen Cross Publications, 1978.

Corbin, Henry. *Creative Imagination in the Sufism of Ibn 'Arabî*. Princeton: Princeton University Press, 1969.

Cummings, E. E. *73 Poems*. London: Faber and Faber, 1974.

Ernst, Carl. *Sufism*. Boston: Shambhala, 1997.

Eliot, T.S. *Four Quartets*. London: Faber and Faber, 1944.

—. *Collected Poems*. London: Faber and Faber, 1963.

Guillaumont A., H.-Ch. Puech, G. Quispel, W. Till, and Yassah 'Abd Al Masih, trans. The Gospel According to Thomas. New York, Hagerstown, San Francisco, London: Harper & Row, 1959.

Hafiz. *I Heard God Laughing*. Trans. Daniel Ladinsky. Walnut Creek: Sufism Reoriented, 1996.

Harvey, Andrew. *Light Upon Light*. Berkeley: North Atlantic Books, 1996.

Hirtenstein, Stephen. *The Unlimited Mercifier*. Ashland, Oregon: White Cloud Press, 1999.

Holy Bible. Authorized Version. London: 1611.

Ibn 'Arabî. *Treatise on Being* (*Risale-t-ul-wujudiyya*). Abingdon, Oxon: Beshara Publications, 1976.

Jami. *Yusuf and Zulaikha*. Trans. David Pendlebury. London: Octagon Press, 1980.

Jung, C. G. *Collected Works*. London: Routledge & Kegan Paul.

—. *Memories, Dreams, Reflections*. London: Flamingo, 1983.

Lao-Tzu. *The Complete Works of Lao Tzu*. Trans. Hua-Ching Ni. Los Angeles: Seven Star, 1979.

Nurbakhsh, Javad. *Sufi Symbolism* vol. I–IV. London: Khaniqahi-Nimatullahi Publications, 1984–1990.

Rashahât 'Ain al-Hayât. *Beads of Dew From the Source of Life*. Fort Lauderdale: Al-Baz Publications, 2001.

Reps, Paul. *Zen Flesh, Zen Bones*. Boston: Tuttle Publishing, 1957.

Rumi. *Delicious Laughter*. Trans. Coleman Barks. Athens, GA: Maypop Books, 1990.

—. *One-Handed Basket Weaving*. Trans. Coleman Barks. Athens, GA: Maypop Books, 1991.

Vaughan-Lee, Llewellyn. *The Signs of God*. Inverness, California: Golden Sufi Center, 2001.

—. *Working with Oneness*. Inverness, California: Golden Sufi Center, 2002.

Yeats, W. B. trans. (with Shree Purohit Swami). *The Ten Principal Upanishads*. London: Faber and Faber, 1937.

INDEX

ACKNOWLEDGMENTS

For permission to use copyrighted material, the author gratefully wishes to acknowledge: Andrew Harvey and North Atlantic Books, for permission to quote from *Light Upon Light: Inspirations from Rumi* by Andrew Harvey (1996); Maypop Books, for permission to quote from *Delicious Laughter*, translations of Rumi by Coleman Barks (1990) and *One-Handed Basket Weaving*, translations of Rumi by Coleman Barks (1991); Daniel Ladinsky, for permission to quote from *I Heard God Laughing: Renderings of Hafiz*, copyright © 1996 Daniel Ladinsky (1996); Khaniqahi Nimatullahi Publications, for permission to quote from *Sufi Symbolism, Vol. I* by Javad Nurbakhsh (1984); Harcourt, Inc., for permission to quote from Part V from "The Hollow Men" in *Collected Poems 1909-1962* by T.S. Eliot, © 1936 by Harcourt, Inc., copyright © 1964, 1963 by T.S. Eliot; Charles E. Tuttle Co., Inc. of Boston, Massachusetts and Tokyo, Japan, for permission to quote from *Zen Flesh, Zen Bones* by Paul Reps (1957); Princeton University Press for permission to quote from *Alone with the Alone: Creative Imagination in the Sufism of Ibn 'Arabî* by Henry Corbin (1969); Seven Star Communications, for permission to quote from pages 28, 51, and 144, *The Complete Works of Lao Tzu, Tao Teh Ching & Hua Hu Ching,* by Hua-Ching Ni © 1979, 1995, www.sevenstarcom.com, taostar@taostar.com; Liveright Publishing Corporation, for permission to quote lines from "one winter afternoon" copyright © 1960, 1988, 1991 by the Trustees for the E. E. Cummings Trust, from *Complete Poems: 1904-1962* by E. E. Cummings, edited by George J. Firmage; and Shambhala Publications, Inc., Boston, for permission to quote from *The Shambhala Guide to Sufism* by Carl W. Ernst, © 1997, www.shambhala.com.

ABOUT *the* AUTHOR

LLEWELLYN VAUGHAN-LEE, Ph.D., is a Sufi Teacher in the Naqshbandiyya-Mujaddidiyya Sufi Order. Born in London in 1953, he has followed the Naqshbandi Sufi path since he was 19. In 1991 he moved to Northern California and became the successor of Irina Tweedie, author of *Chasm of Fire* and *Daughter of Fire*. In recent years the focus of his writing and teaching has been on spiritual responsibility in our present time of transition, and the emerging global consciousness of oneness (see www.workingwithoneness.org). He has also specialized in the area of dreamwork, integrating the ancient Sufi approach to dreams with the insights of modern psychology. Author of several books, Llewellyn lectures throughout the United States and Europe.

ABOUT *the* PUBLISHER

THE GOLDEN SUFI CENTER is a California Religious Non-Profit Corporation dedicated to making the teachings of the Naqshbandi Sufi path available to all seekers. For further information about the activities and publications, please contact:

THE GOLDEN SUFI CENTER
P.O. Box 428
Inverness, CA 94937-0428
tel: 415-663-8773 · *fax:* 415-663-9128
info@goldensufi.org · www.goldensufi.org

ABOUT WORKING *with* ONENESS

www.workingwithoneness.org

This site is dedicated to connecting with spiritual groups of all types who are working towards the emerging consciousness of oneness. Consciousness of oneness is an awareness of the unity and interconnectedness of all of life. This is central to our human and planetary survival and evolution.

At the present time there is a greater need for those of us drawn to this work of oneness to connect with each other. We hope this website will be a valuable resource for you in facilitating this connection.

Please visit our website, www.workingwithoneness.org
or contact us at info@workingwithoneness.org.